LIBERTY AND POWER

THE PEW FORUM DIALOGUES
ON RELIGION AND PUBLIC LIFE

E.J. DIONNE JR., JEAN BETHKE ELSHTAIN, KAYLA M. DROGOSZ

Series Editors

THE PEW
FORUM
ON RELIGION
& PUBLIC LIFE

This book series is a joint project of the Pew Forum on Religion and Public Life and the Brookings Institution.

The Forum (www.pewforum.org) seeks to promote a deeper understanding of issues at the intersection of religion and public affairs by delivering timely, impartial information to national opinion leaders, including federal government officials, journalists, policy analysts and national advocacy organizations. As a nonpartisan, non-advocacy organization, the Forum does not take positions on policy debates.

The Pew Forum Dialogues on Religion and Public Life are short volumes that bring together the voices of scholars, journalists and policy leaders engaged simultaneously in the religious and policy realms. The core idea behind the dialogues is a simple one: There are many authentically expert voices addressing important public questions who speak not only from their knowledge of the policy issues but also from a set of moral concerns that are often shaped by their religious commitments. Our goal is to deepen public understanding of the issues by inviting these voices to join in a dialogue.

Based in Washington, D.C., the Forum is directed by Luis Lugo. The Forum is a project of the Pew Research Center.

OTHER TITLES IN THIS SERIES

Is the Market Moral? A Dialogue on Religion, Economics, and Justice
Rebecca M. Blank and William McGurn

Lifting Up the Poor: A Dialogue on Religion, Poverty, and Welfare Reform
Mary Jo Bane and Lawrence M. Mead

One Electorate under God? A Dialogue on Religion and American Politics
Mario Cuomo, Mark Souder, and others

LIBERTY AND POWER

A DIALOGUE ON RELIGION AND U.S. FOREIGN POLICY IN AN UNJUST WORLD

J. BRYAN HEHIR

MICHAEL WALZER

LOUISE RICHARDSON

SHIBLEY TELHAMI

CHARLES KRAUTHAMMER

JAMES LINDSAY

BROOKINGS INSTITUTION PRESS
Washington, D.C.

ABOUT BROOKINGS

The Brookings Institution is a private nonprofit organization devoted to research, education, and publication on important issues of domestic and foreign policy. Its principal purpose is to bring knowledge to bear on current and emerging policy problems. The Institution maintains a position of neutrality on issues of public policy. Interpretations or conclusions in Brookings publications should be understood to be solely those of the authors.

Library of Congress Cataloging-in-Publication data
Liberty and power : a dialogue on religion and U.S. foreign policy in an unjust world / J. Bryan Hehir . . . [et al.].
   p.   cm   —(The Pew Forum dialogues on religion and public life)
   Includes bibliographical references and index.
   ISBN 0-8157-3545-6 (pbk. : alk. paper)
   1. United States—Foreign relations—Moral and ethical aspects.
2. Religion and international affairs. 3. War (International law)
I. Hehir, J. Bryan. II. Title. III. Series.
   JZ1480.L53 2004
   205'.624—dc22   2004019511

2 4 6 8 9 7 5 3 1

The paper used in this publication meets minimum requirements of the American National Standard for Information Sciences—Permanence of Paper for Printed Library Materials: ANSI Z39.48-1992.

Typeset in Adobe Caslon

Composition by R. Lynn Rivenbark
Macon, Georgia

Printed by Victor Graphics
Baltimore, Maryland

CONTENTS

Contents

FOREWORD

From the founding fathers on, many Americans have thought of themselves as citizens of a Christian nation. But the United States has always been a melting pot society; the "pluribus" in its motto includes religious diversity, and its Constitution insists on the separation of church and state. In the 1950s Will Herberg titled his classic *Protestant-Catholic-Jew: An Essay in American Religious Sociology*, which laid much of the intellectual groundwork for the introduction of the "civil religion" thesis a decade later. If updated today, it would have to be called *Protestant, Catholic, Jew, Muslim, Buddhist, Hindu, Sikh*. And that would not be a complete list. In fact, it should probably include *Humanist, Agnostic, and Atheist* and a handful of other categories as well.

Instead, we have the book before you now. Its title is simpler, but the reality it deals with is no less complex. The editors—my Brookings colleagues, E. J. Dionne Jr. and Kayla M. Drogosz, and Jean Bethke Elshtain of the University of Chicago—are, respectively, Catholic, Jewish, and Protestant. They admit their interest in the subject of religion and its role in public life and public policy is personal, and it is also animated by their commitment to democratic politics and the serious study of religion in America.

In the pages that follow they hope to open the debate in areas where lines are drawn hard and fast. *Liberty and Power* is based on the idea that we can learn from others who have strong religious convictions, whether or not we share their faith and, to paraphrase Isaiah Berlin, that ideas matter, not just as products of the intellect but as guides to governance and inspirations of democratic culture.

While there are differences among both the editors and the contributors, they share a conviction that good citizenship in a democracy need not conflict with theological convictions.

Two of the series editors, E. J. and Jean, are accomplished scholars of religion and politics and together helped found and co-chair the Pew Forum on Religion and Public Life. Kayla, who has helped shape each volume in the series, understands how religion and public commitments can strengthen bonds and create common things. She serves as the senior research analyst in Governance Studies at Brookings and as a visiting faculty fellow with the Center for Democracy and the Third Sector at Georgetown University.

The purpose of the Pew Forum dialogues is not to impress a particular viewpoint on readers, and it is certainly not to suggest that there is only one answer to any of the questions posed. These dialogues are intended to open the debate, not to close it. At the same time, the editors and authors here remained concerned with the tough questions of how to develop prudent public policy and foster democratic culture. We are grateful for the support of the Pew Charitable Trusts and the Pew Forum on Religion and Public Life, which are committed to an expanded effort to bring policy experts and civic leaders together to discuss the relationship between religion and politics.

The first two volumes in the Pew Forum Dialogues on Religion and Public Life series, *Lifting Up the Poor: A Dialogue on Religion, Poverty, and Welfare Reform*, by Mary Jo Bane and Lawrence M. Mead, and *Is the Market Moral? A Dialogue on Religion, Economics, and Justice*, by Rebecca M. Blank and William McGurn, engage experts in a clear, open, and honest discussion of how their faith influences their understanding of tough policy choices on domestic policy issues. The third book, *One Electorate under God? A Dialogue on Religion and American Politics*, is a selection of essays from politicians, journalists, and academics seeking to promote a greater understanding of American thinking about faith and public office in a pluralistic society.

This fourth volume in the dialogue series explores a point largely excluded from the public discourse thus far, that the same religious and moral values that inform our debates about welfare policy, abortion, and other domestic issues also help us understand our obligations to other countries. When President George W. Bush in April 2004 called freedom "the Almighty's gift to the world," and said that it was America's obligation to ensure its spread, his spiritual reference underscored the need for a debate on the religious and ethical foundations of America's conduct outside its own borders.

Liberty and Power centers around essays from two of the foremost scholars of theology, politics, and morality: Bryan Hehir and Michael Walzer. Bryan Hehir is formerly the president and CEO of Catholic Charities USA and is currently professor of the practice of religion and public life at Harvard's Kennedy School of Government. Michael Walzer is a professor of social science at the Institute for Advanced Study at Princeton University and is author or coeditor of more than a dozen books on just war, political theory, and social ethics.

In their contributions, the two primary authors draw from contrasting faith and moral traditions to reach many of the same conclusions. Hehir approaches the topic through the scope of his Catholic background, discussing the role of Reinhold Niebuhr and just war theory in twentieth-century American foreign affairs, and building on their principles to advocate a modest foreign policy: multilateralism over unilateralism, and deterrence over preemptive war.

Walzer draws his arguments primarily from moral grounds, which he quips "is perhaps a Jewish strategy for dealing with these matters." He argues in these pages that much of the wisdom on the subject of war and foreign aid is "accumulated human wisdom," not rooted in divine authority, and that the doctrine of multilateralism and deterrence that he subscribes to is a broad moral idea, not a narrow religious one. "Even people who work within religious traditions," he says, "should never lay claim to, should never be allowed to lay claim to, divine authority." Faith-based foreign policy, he cautions, doesn't always foster reasonable decisionmaking.

The four essays that follow are responses from foreign policy experts with diverse perspectives, displaying an extraordinary breadth and depth of ideas that complement and critique the two central essays. Charles Krauthammer is a former political speech writer and a Pulitzer Prize–winning syndicated columnist for the *Washington Post* Writers Group. Jim

Lindsay is a vice president at the Council on Foreign Relations and was previously a senior fellow at the Brookings Institution and a member of the National Security Council under President Clinton. Louise Richardson is an expert in international terrorism and defense policy and currently serves as the executive dean of the Radcliffe Institute for Advanced Study at Harvard University. Shibley Telhami serves as nonresident senior fellow at the Brookings Institution and is the Anwar Sadat Professor for Peace and Development at the University of Maryland.

While all the authors provide nuanced responses to the central essays, Krauthammer provides the sharpest critique of the multilateralism and deterrence advocated by Hehir and Walzer. Drawing on realist philosophy, he argues that international consensus itself does not provide legitimacy and that the threats present in a post–September 11th world necessitate a policy of what he terms "preemptive intervention."

As the contributors to this volume show, the public obligations of faith are an essential and enduring part of the American experiment. Our hope in publishing this book is that the essays will spark a renewed national discussion on a topic that will be relevant for a long time to come.

As always with the product of a project of this kind, a disclaimer is in order: the opinions expressed in this volume are those of the authors alone and do not necessarily reflect the views of the Pew Forum, the Pew Charitable Trusts, or the trustees, officers, or staff of the Brookings Institution. That said, *Liberty and Power* fits perfectly with the Brookings tradition of independent, open-minded, nonpartisan public policy research on important national and international topics. In exploring the complexities of faith, morals, and foreign policy, it combines serious scholarship with the insights of policy practitioners committed to democratic practice.

STROBE TALBOTT
President, Brookings Institution

August 2004
Washington, D.C.

ACKNOWLEDGMENTS

THE PEW FORUM DIALOGUES on Religion and Public Life, through fortune and the help of many people named below, have consistently obtained contributions from the most serious political thinkers who enrich the discussion of religious issues. This volume is the fourth in a series that is a creation of the Pew Forum on Religion and Public Life. They are also a part of its expanded efforts to bring policy experts and civic leaders together to discuss the relationship between faith, politics, and public life.

This book, like much that bears the Brookings imprint, is the result of collaboration. The editors are extremely grateful to Strobe Talbott, president of the Brookings Institution, for his deep and energetic commitment to this project; to Pietro Nivola for his leadership as the new director of Brookings's Governance Studies program; to Tom Mann, Paul Light, and Carol Graham for their friendship and for doing so much to make our projects possible; to Katherine Moore for helping in countless way to bring this series to life; to Bethany Hase for administrative assistance; to our superb interns Dan Treglia and Rachel Kreinces, who diligently helped pull the final pieces of this project together and who brightened each day of our week; to Robert Faherty, the director of the Brookings Institution Press, who never fails us, embraces our projects, and always offers wise advice; to John Sherer and Nicole Pagano for making sure that this publication saw the light of day and made it into the right hands at just the right time; to Janet Walker and Theresa Walker for being patient, careful, and kind editors; to Carlotta Ribar for proofreading; and to Susan

Woollen and Sese Paul Design for creating such a striking cover design for this book and for the other volumes in the dialogue series.

We are also grateful to Rebecca Rimel, the president of the Pew Charitable Trusts, and Luis Lugo, who served as the director of its religion program and is now the director of the Pew Forum on Religion and Public Life. Without their leadership, vision, and support, much of our work on religion and public life at Brookings simply would not exist. Luis Lugo always offers creative suggestions and excellent advice. He has a steadfast commitment to the most serious research in the area of religion and politics. Luis is deeply knowledgeable and cares passionately about the issues at the core of the Pew Forum and this dialogue series. We are grateful to him.

We are blessed to have worked with Melissa Rogers, who served as the Pew Forum's first executive director and whose leadership helped shape the Forum since the beginning. We are also indebted to Sandy Stencel. As the Forum's associate director, Sandy works with warmth, understanding, and much patience, and we're grateful for all the talents she brings to all our projects. We are grateful as well to all our other colleagues at the Pew Forum.

Above all, we owe a tremendous debt to our authors. Careful arguments about how religious principles affect foreign policy are rare enough. Father Bryan Hehir, Michael Walzer, Charles Krauthammer, Jim Lindsay, Louise Richardson, and Shibley Telhami are the best in their respective fields, and they are exceptional colleagues. They bring to the discussion years of experience, and their carefully argued perspectives complement and question each other, producing a discourse infinitely more valuable than the sum of each individual's contribution.

LIBERTY AND POWER

THE PARADOXES OF RELIGION
AND FOREIGN POLICY
AN INTRODUCTION

E.J. DIONNE JR., KAYLA M. DROGOSZ, AND JEAN BETHKE ELSHTAIN

BRINGING RELIGION into international relations scares people, especially after the attacks of September 11, 2001. It also seems a new departure, even if it is not. As J. Bryan Hehir notes in his pathbreaking essay in these pages, the dominant attitude over the last half century on the subject was expressed well by Dean Acheson, Harry Truman's secretary of state. "Moral Talk was fine preaching for the Final Day of Judgment," Acheson said, "but it was not a view I would entertain as a public servant."

A lot of public servants and foreign policy analysts feel that way. As Louise Richardson notes herein, "The arguments on the basis of moral obligation are entirely convincing when they are preached to the choir, but they fall on deaf ears when they are proposed to the policymakers."

James Lindsay agrees strongly with Hehir on the need to "think a lot more about the impact of religion on world politics." But Lindsay adds, rightly, "This is going to be hard to do. We are not used to thinking about the topic. We do not have much practice handling religion, and the consequences of getting it wrong could be enormous." Indeed.

The unease over introducing religion into foreign affairs is rooted in two fears. The first is that it can be a conversation stopper and retard rather than advance an honest discussion of morality. "In the contemporary world," writes Michael Walzer, perhaps the nation's premier student

1

of just war, "I suggest that we need to worry about faith—for when it turns into dogma and certainty, as it frequently does, it tends to override morality." Walzer concludes: "A faith-based foreign policy is a bad idea."

Lindsay expresses sympathy for "the tendency of Americans to cast their foreign policy preferences in moral terms." But he adds, "That tendency . . . can squelch debate. When people become certain of their moral rectitude, they can easily drift into sanctimony, so anybody who disagrees with them must, by definition, not be really interested in moral issues. That attitude tends to poison debate rather than advance it." Of course, one must note that realpolitik—if it hardens into dogma—similarly quashes debate and brooks no opposition.

Charles Krauthammer is even more direct in his rejection of religion's utility as a guide to "a moral foreign policy." He writes, "Religion as an abstraction will not tell, inform, or guide anyone about how to act collectively or individually."

The second fear is rooted in the bloody history of wars over religion in past centuries and in today's acts of terrorism that are often justified in religious terms. Hehir provides a useful and important history of the Westphalian synthesis, created by the 1648 Treaty of Westphalia. It recognized the emergence of the modern sovereign state in order to "move decisively beyond the century of religious warfare that had ravaged European politics." Under the Westphalian synthesis, political actors would stop using religious differences as reasons for interfering in the affairs of territories under the rule of others. "Sovereignty," Hehir writes, "meant a defined territory, an effective exercise of authority within the territory and—a decisive change—the refusal of the sovereign to recognize any superior authority, temporal or spiritual." A key moment in the birth of the idea of "separating church and state" was that treaty.

There is a great fear, especially among foreign policy realists, that the abandonment of the Westphalian synthesis will invite a return to the religious wars of old. Walzer, for his part, fears that "just war" theories might be displaced by a "faith-based" model. He writes, "There is an alternative tradition, a medieval rival of just war, which has not been wholly supplanted: the crusade, the holy war, the jihad. All these words describe a faith-based struggle against the forces of darkness and evil, which are generally understood in explicitly religious terms: infidels, idolaters, the antichrist. In the West, especially after 9/11, we are a little leery about holy wars."

So are religious principles a blessing or a curse in guiding our understanding of relations among states and nations? The most popular answer—"Well, it depends"—is not necessarily the most helpful, though it may be the most honest. It depends upon which religious principles, how they are applied, and what questions they purport to answer or problems they address. And Shibley Telhami is absolutely right when he suggests that the discussion of the relationship of religion to politics (domestic as well as international) is confusing because too little effort is made to differentiate "between the role of religious ideas and the role of religious organizations." It is clearly the case, as Telhami points out, that the African American church was essential in building the civil rights movement, just as the Roman Catholic Church in Poland was essential in organizing opposition to that country's Communist dictatorship in the 1970s and 1980s. In each case, Christian ideas were mobilized on behalf of a just cause. But in each case, as well, the sheer organizational power of the churches—and the fact that the church was one of the few available institutions in which independent political action could be rooted—was at least as important.

Because the questions at stake on this subject are so vexing *and* so urgent, the editors of this series are especially grateful to the exceptional thinkers who accepted our invitation to join in this dialogue. This volume is the fourth in a series that is a joint project of the Pew Forum on Religion and Public Life and the Brookings Institution. The series is based on a simple proposition, one that its editors see as obvious but that others might see as controversial: Religious voices and insights rooted in faith have a great deal to contribute to our public deliberations about politics and public policy. As our coeditor Jean Bethke Elshtain says, "American politics is indecipherable if it is severed from the interplay and panoply of America's religions."[1] The same is increasingly true of world politics.

The series is also rooted in the idea that religious people—including people who share the same faith and live the same religious tradition—can disagree fundamentally on political questions not only because they see the facts differently, but also because they read and experience their traditions differently. The series emphatically rejects the idea that faith commitments render the messy facts about politics and policy irrelevant. On the contrary, we sought out people of faith who respect the facts and have genuine knowledge of the issues about which they speak.

The first volume of the series, *Lifting Up the Poor: A Dialogue on Religion, Poverty, and Welfare Reform*, brings together in dialogue Mary Jo Bane and Lawrence M. Mead, two of the nation's premier experts on poverty and welfare policy. Both care profoundly about the facts—and their faith. In *Is the Market Moral? A Dialogue on Religion, Economics, and Justice*, Rebecca M. Blank and William McGurn show how their reflections on economics, rooted in years of engagement with the subject, interact with their moral commitments rooted in faith. Bane and Mead, Blank and McGurn all perform a service in demonstrating that faith speaks to questions that are not easily pigeonholed as religious issues. And they provide a model in demonstrating the obligations of the person of faith in the public realm: They make arguments accessible and engaging to those who may not share their particular brands of faith, their specific approaches to theology. The third volume, *One Electorate under God?* takes on the broad question of the relationship between faith and American politics. Anchored in a discussion between former New York governor Mario Cuomo and Representative Mark Souder of Indiana—they reflect on the role of faith in their own political lives—the volume brings together a wide array of voices on a set of questions that relate to but also transcend the sharp debates of a particular election year.

The inspiration behind the series is captured in that earlier volume by Martha Minow, a professor at Harvard Law School. "Religiously inflected arguments and perspectives bring critical and prophetic insight and energy to politics and public affairs." There is, she says, "something woefully lacking in any view that excludes religion entirely from the public sphere." Yet one can believe this and still accept that "difficulties arise if government actions cross over from reflecting religious sources of vision and energy to preferring one kind of religion over others." And Lord knows (if one may invoke the Almighty in this context), that is especially true in foreign policy and in relations among states.

This volume began taking shape in February 2003, when we invited five of our authors to a meeting at which they were asked to discuss faith, morals, and foreign policy. (Shibley Telhami, who did not attend that session, was later invited to join the discussion, and we are very grateful he has.) We gave the participants a list of questions—some of them refer to these questions in the text—to open, though not limit, the discussion. Hehir and Walzer were asked to give lengthy reflections. The other authors were asked to respond to them, though we also asked them not to be shy about pushing the discussion in any direction they thought helpful. (Fortunately, this is not a shy group.) The timing of the original event in some ways sharpened the debate, since the meeting was held at the moment when the United States was preparing to go to war in Iraq. We later asked our authors to use their remarks as the basis for the essays here. They were put in final form early in 2004.

We are biased, perhaps, but we think we have brought together some of our country's most powerful voices on this topic. J. Bryan Hehir has devoted his life to combining the roles of a committed diocesan priest, a prominent scholar on international affairs, and one of the nation's leading moral voices on foreign policy. He came to wide attention for his work as a policy adviser at the U.S. Catholic Conference. A principal author of the bishops' famous pastoral letter on nuclear weapons, *The Challenge of Peace,* Hehir has remained active in politics and foreign policy and exerted enormous influence on the policy agenda that the American bishops pursued. "Being engaged with the world has been a major emphasis in my life. I wanted to go into politics," he says, "before I went into the ministry. I was sure I wanted to study diplomacy before I knew I wanted to study theology."[2] Hehir is seen by many Catholics—and many non-Catholics as well—as a successor to the American Jesuit John Courtney Murray, the leading Catholic theologian and intellectual of his day.[3] As noted in these pages, the late Reinhold Niebuhr's theological insights proved so valuable to those who did not share his faith that a group of intellectuals came to describe themselves informally as Atheists for Niebuhr. A comparable group no doubt exists where Bryan Hehir is concerned, even as his deep religious faith shines through all of his work.

Michael Walzer has grappled with these questions throughout an extraordinary life that has bridged the worlds of philosophical reflection and political commitment. One of his first major works, *The Revolution of the Saints,* explores the interaction of religious faith and revolutionary politics in the time of Oliver Cromwell. It still stands as a model for understanding the interplay between realms so often treated separately. Walzer's *Just and Unjust Wars* continues to stand as a definitive discussion of the subject. He has been at work on a multivolume collection on Jewish political philosophy. And his *Exodus and Revolution* is a powerful reminder of how tradition can be usefully studied and invoked, generation after generation, to illuminate contemporary dilemmas and to inspire right action. Since 1980 he has been a member of the Institute for Advanced Study at Princeton, where he has written some of the best-known books on moral philosophy, social criticism, Jewish political theory, and politics. Perhaps most important, Walzer, like Hehir, is admired for his ability to marry sustained political commitment with a moral outlook that is not inhibited or limited by ideology and that is open to insights from other shores, intellectual as well as geographic.

With the Hehir and Walzer chapters the bedrock of this collection, our respondents did, indeed, do far more than respond. They offered creative alternative views of their own and helped highlight central themes of this volume: the role of realism in foreign policy, the relationship between realism and other views rooted in moral and religious traditions, and the ways in which globalization and nonstate actors (including terrorists) call into question old paradigms of foreign relations.

Louise Richardson, the senior administrative officer of the Radcliffe Institute for Advanced Study, has written widely on terrorism and ethnic conflict. She has a profound understanding of the darker side of politics. Her most recent research focuses on a study of decisionmaking inside terrorist organizations and patterns of terrorist violence.

Shibley Telhami, who has a long association with the Brookings Institution and is a professor at the University of Maryland, is a distinguished scholar of the Middle East. Many know he is a political scientist, but few know he also has a graduate degree in philosophy and religion from the Graduate Theological Union in Berkeley, where he studied Judaism, Christianity, and Islam and their connection to politics. Shibley can reach to his own biography to understand ethnic and religious conflict— and the inspirations that faith can offer. A Christian Arab, he was born in Haifa, Israel. He identifies with being called both a Palestinian Arab and an Arab Israeli and has been active in encouraging a peaceful resolution to the Arab-Israeli conflict. His fair-mindedness and analytical independence is well reflected in his recent book, *The Stakes: America and the Middle East.*

James Lindsay, a vice president at the Council on Foreign Relations and before that a colleague of ours at Brookings, is a premier student of contemporary foreign policy and a powerful voice in contemporary debates. Having served as a consultant to the Hart-Rudmann Commission, he is, like Richardson, well versed in the politics of terrorism. With Ivo Daalder, he is the author of *America Unbound,* widely seen as the definitive first look at the Bush administration's foreign policy.

And Charles Krauthammer is a well-known (and Pulitzer Prize–winning) syndicated columnist who invented the idea of a Reagan Doctrine and is one of the most important interpreters of the realist approach to foreign policy. Krauthammer, whose publications include *Cutting Edges: Making Sense of the Eighties,* provides, as readers will discover, a powerful counterpoint to some of the perspectives offered by Hehir, Walzer, and Telhami in particular. Krauthammer's very skepticism of the project embodied in this book makes his an especially important—and at times, puckish—voice. With candor, he writes, "I am sure one can find any message one seeks in the Bible, depending on where one looks."

Well, yes, but. . . . As the essays here show, it is certainly possible for political actors to fish out from scripture or tradition whatever arguments might accommodate their interests. But serious students of morality and foreign policy—and certainly serious students of tradition—often find themselves disciplined, intellectually and morally, by the traditions from which they spring. And it is not at all surprising that those who share a tradition (or think they do) can disagree profoundly about the implications of that tradition for contemporary action. Walzer, we think, has it exactly right when he says, "Traditions are sites for arguments, and that's not less true of religious than of secular traditions." Reinhold Niebuhr, whose name rightly appears often in these pages, took sharp issue with his pacifist Christian colleagues in the years before World War II, even as both invoked the same scriptures to make their respective cases.

Invoking Niebuhr is a reminder of our country's rich tradition of ethical and religious reflection on foreign affairs. Hehir's essay notes that the "Christian realist" tradition has long jostled with ideas rooted in Catholic natural law theory and that Pope John XXIII's encyclical *Pacem in Terris*

(*Peace on Earth*) had a powerful impact on the American debate. Niebuhr also stands as a trenchant counterpoint to those who would claim that religious voices and religious arguments lead inevitably to overreaching and arrogant certainty. On the contrary, as Richard Fox, one of Niebuhr's leading interpreters, has said, one of the great theologian's primary lessons is the need for humility. Niebuhr, Fox says, asserted repeatedly that an "awareness of sin—of one's often hidden desire for fame, power, privilege, and other kinds of self-aggrandizement—can counteract religious people's temptation to see themselves as chosen instruments for divinely sponsored action."[4]

This is just one of the many paradoxes—or should one say *seeming* paradoxes?—explored in these pages. Other paradoxes emerge in the complicated relationship between realist arguments and moral arguments. On one side, Walzer tells the fascinating story of the arguments within the British government over the strategic bombing campaign against Germany during World War II. The question at the time was whether the goal of the campaign should be "to kill as many German civilians as possible, so as to demoralize the enemy and shut down the economy, or should the planes aim only at military targets—railroad yards, tank factories, and army bases." As Walzer argues, both sides made their case entirely in practical terms. "Inside the government, there seemed to be a ban on moral talk: there's no one here but us realists!" Yet when one examines the postwar political and moral commitments of the partisans on each side, "it seems clear that their moral and political convictions—most crucially, their views about the rightness or wrongness of killing enemy civilians—had driven their wartime arguments." We are accustomed to moralism as a cover for realism. We are less sensitive to the way in which arguments seemingly rooted in a realist tradition are in fact surrogates for moral or even religious commitments.

From a slightly different angle, Shibley Telhami makes the case that nations that root their behavior in morality often find that morality also has highly practical uses—or as Telhami puts it, "A strong instrumental argument can be made on behalf of international ethical behavior." For example, stopping terrorism is a central goal of the United States' foreign policy. But the core argument against terrorism, as Telhami writes, is *moral*—"the ends, no matter how worthy, cannot justify the means"—and "boils down to the notion that deliberate attack on civilian targets is unacceptable under any circumstances." The key, he says, is that "to persuade others of this worthy notion, those who make the argument must speak with moral authority." To boil down Telhami's case: To achieve the practical end of eradicating or reducing terrorism, the United States needs moral authority on its side, an authority that can ultimately be won only through moral action.

This book appears at a moment of great contention in foreign policy, and readers should know that all the authors here closely link their ideas and their arguments to the very practical issues that confront us: the costs and benefits of preemptive and preventive war (and the differences between the two); the advisability (or lack thereof) of the United States' intervention in Iraq; the obligations created by the United States' unprecedented military advantages (and the dangers thereof); the best ways of judging when "humanitarian" interventions are feasible, moral, necessary—and, yes, genuinely humanitarian.

It is possible, of course, for those who care about international relations to minimize their engagement with issues rooted in religion. But we would assert, with Hehir, that it is not possible even for the clearest-eyed realist to avoid grappling with the importance of religious forces in shaping the world as it now exists. And we are certain that those who *are* religious cannot possibly avoid the questions raised here. At the very least, religious people need to question themselves to make sure that what they see as religious imperatives are not in fact cloaks for other interests. It is always possible, as Telhami puts it, that "one may be having a delusion, not hearing the real voice of God."

The obligation of religious people to engage the world was put most pointedly by Dietrich Bonhoeffer, the anti-Nazi theologian who was imprisoned for his part in a plot to assassinate Hitler and later killed. Bonhoeffer judges harshly those who retreat into the "sanctuary of private virtuousness" when confronted with hideous injustice. "Anyone who does this must shut his mouth and his eyes to the injustices around him," Bonhoeffer writes. "Responsible action involves contamination—one cannot altogether avoid getting 'dirty hands' when acting in the political world in responsible ways."[5]

But how dirty—and bloody—must one's hands get? At what point does the contamination of which Bonhoeffer speaks become a threat to the responsible action to which he rightly calls us? Ultimately, these are the questions with which our authors grapple. In an imperfect world, they are the questions that all people of faith, and also those without faith, must inevitably confront.

Notes

1. Jean Bethke Elshtain, "God Talk and the Citizen-Believer," from *One Electorate under God? A Dialogue on Religion and American Politics*, edited by E. J. Dionne Jr., Jean Bethke Elshtain, and Kayla M. Drogosz (Brookings, 2004), p. 94.

2. J. Bryan Hehir, "Catholic Theology at Its Best," *Harvard Divinity Bulletin* 27, nos. 2–3 (1998): 13.

3. See also William J. Gould, "Father J. Bryan Hehir: Priest, Policy Analyst, and Theologian of Dialogue," in *Religious Leaders and Faith-Based Politics*, edited by Jo Renee Formicola and Hubert Morken (Oxford, U.K.: Rowman and Littlefield, 2001).

4. Richard Wightman Fox, "The Politics of Religion in a Sinful World," in *One Electorate under God? A Dialogue on Religion and American Politics*, edited by E. J. Dionne Jr., Jean Bethke Elshtain, and Kayla M. Drogosz (Brookings, 2004), pp. 96–97.

5. See Dietrich Bonhoeffer, *Letters and Papers from Prison* (New York: Collier Books, 1971), pp. 4–5. See also Jean Bethke Elshtain, *Just War against Terror: The Burden of American Power in a Violent World* (New York: Basic Books, 2003).

RELIGION, REALISM, AND JUST INTERVENTION

J. BRYAN HEHIR

Even thirty years ago the topic "faith, morals, and public policy" would not have been a normal topic for reflection among both foreign policy elites and the general public. Certainly, one could explore, at any moment in the history of the republic, the relationship of faith and politics, religion, and public policy, but discussion would have occurred under religious auspices or in certain academic centers, not in a premier Washington think tank.

For most of the past fifty years the dominant attitude, expressed in Dean Acheson's words, might have been "Moral Talk was fine preaching for the Final Day of Judgment, but it was not a view I would entertain as a public servant."[1]

The recognition that Acheson's view is inadequate today has been driven by events. Like it or not, it is now almost impossible to isolate or insulate foreign policy and world politics from the normative convictions and categories embodied in the phrase "faith and morals." Recognizing the need to relate these themes, however, yields little guidance on how to do so skillfully. For many the desire to keep religion and morality separate from analysis of politics, strategy, and economics has been grounded in a conviction that the effort to relate them yields confusion, not illumination, that the risks entailed are disproportionate to expected benefits, and that dealing with "the facts" of world politics is daunting enough without seeking also to be virtuous about it.

Nonetheless, today the effort is worth the risk, and my attempt to tackle it is organized in three steps: an analysis of the general topic of religion and world politics, examples of how religion, morality, and U.S. foreign policy have been related, and the use of an ethic rooted in a religious tradition to explore the question of war and intervention in the current international system.

Religion and World Politics: A Changed and Changing Agenda

Many authors have narrated the story of how previous conceptions of world politics and foreign policy are being brought under review and revision. I seek only to summarize the story because it poses the background for this discussion.[2]

To begin, the seventeenth-century origin of the story was a *fault line*. Participants stepped beyond the remnants of the medieval order of politics and explicitly recognized the emergence of the modern sovereign state. That might be called the secular side of the narrative. The religious fault line was the effort to move decisively beyond the century of religious warfare that had ravaged European politics. The decline of medieval patterns of political authority and the consequences of the Reformation had created a religious-political struggle that took thousands of lives in wars without restraint.

Daniel Philpott describes the intellectual, diplomatic, and strategic creation fashioned over time to create the modern international order as the "Westphalian synthesis."[3] In some form the content of that synthesis shaped the study and practice of world politics into the middle of the twentieth century. The United Nations modified the synthesis but also depended on its premises. Describing the premises is a contested exercise; I rely on my own effort to state the content of the synthesis but acknowledge that there are variants of this theme.

The synthesis had two explicit propositions and a third implicit idea. The political proposition was the recognition of and support for the sovereign state as the basic unit of world politics. Sovereignty meant a defined territory, an effective exercise of authority within the territory, and—a decisive change—the refusal of the sovereign to recognize any superior authority, temporal or spiritual. The emergence of sovereignty was a process, not an event; the power of the sovereign state developed between the fourteenth and seventeenth century. Its unique role in world politics can be tied to the Westphalian legacy, but it took the following two centuries to consolidate it.

The correlative strategic proposition to sovereignty was the rule of nonintervention. Surely the experience of the religious wars, in which intervention was pursued consistently and destructively, led to the evolving notion that the price of order and security for states was some understanding that sovereign boundaries should be respected. The proposition was built on the basic distinction between the internal life of states and their external conduct. The nonintervention principle sought to remove the internal affairs of states from the possible reasons for war. The political, religious, and social order of states might vary greatly but should not constitute a *casus belli*. A contemporary advocate of the Westphalian synthesis, Henry Kissinger, describes the intent of this principle: "The Treaty of Westphalia reflected a general determination to put an end to carnage once and for all. Its basic purpose (in modern terms) was to stop the merging of domestic and foreign policy (in the language of the period) of faith and diplomacy."[4]

Kissinger's description closes with the third element of the Westphalian synthesis, the determination to secularize world politics, again to remove religion as a *casus belli*. The first two principles, sovereignty and nonintervention, are explicitly invoked in any modern description of international relations. They are the threshold principles of participation in the United Nations. The third, religious, principle is often simply assumed. The separation of religion from political discourse and the broader assumption that religion may be treated as a "private phenomenon," significant in the lives of individuals but not a force of public consequence, has been treated as a given in the discipline of international relations and in the discourse of foreign policy. The effect of this broadly based assumption has been evident in the scant reference to religious themes in the analysis of world politics and the absence of any bureaucratic or institutional attention paid to religious institutions or traditions in the diplomacy of states.

Crossing the fault line means recognizing today that the Westphalian synthesis is still an organizing concept of world politics, but its three elements have all been modified. The sovereign state remains the basic unit of world politics, but the possession of sovereignty by a state does not yield the kind of absolute freedom and control of one's destiny that the formal concept once implied. From economic interdependence to human rights claims to the capacities of transnational actors, the limits on operational sovereignty are evident today. Sovereignty is relative in weight, significance, and control; sovereign states share the stage of history today with other actors and ideas.[5] During the 1990s nonintervention was brought under intellectual scrutiny and diplomatic review. Again, to capture the process through the eyes of a skeptic, the words of Kissinger: "Probably the most dramatic transformation in the nature of contemporary international affairs has been the general acceptance of the proposition that certain universal principles are deemed enforceable either by the United Nations or, in extreme situations, by a group of states."[6]

While he fears this transformation "may usher in a new period of global interventionism with unforseeable consequences," during the past decade many authors and diplomats sought to affirm the value of nonintervention and to define circumstances when it should be overridden in the name of protecting life and defending human rights.[7] Like sovereignty, nonintervention today has, for many, only relative value.[8]

Finally, and most pertinent to this discussion, there is a growing consensus that a complete secularization of world politics, or an analytical effort to divorce religion from the political order, yields a distorted conception of contemporary world politics. There is little support for a collapse of the distinction between the political and religious domains of life. The crossing of the fault line resides in a more modest proposition that the public and social significance of religion, its potential for positive and negative effects on politics, must be given attention and weight. The most recent statement of the case, Philpott's essay "The Challenge of September 11 to Secularism in International Relations," surveys both the events that call the separation into question and the growing body of literature that seeks to bridge the religious and the political, not in a mode of advocacy for religion but simply for the sake of accurate analysis of world politics.

The critique that standard versions of international relations theory or diplomatic engagement have ignored religion is not sufficient. There is now a need for the constructive work of relating religious traditions to world politics in a systematic fashion. It has begun to some degree, but we are in the early stages of the enterprise. The fault line has been crossed in many quarters, but the work ahead is greater than what has been accomplished thus far.

Religion and Foreign Policy: The U.S. Experience

Two pertinent questions are "How do groups with different moral traditions influence the formation of U.S. foreign policy?" and "How should religious and moral tenets guide foreign policy?" Although the separation of religious traditions from the analysis of world politics has been rigorous, the role of religious institutions and communities in the United States has been a frequent factor in the foreign policy debate. Leo P. Ribuffo's essay, "Religion in the History of U.S. Foreign Policy," reviews this interaction.[9] I do not intend to sketch the narrative of this historical question as Ribuffo has helpfully done. Rather I seek to identify examples of distinct positions within the Christian community that have engaged the issue of religion, morality, and foreign policy. Part of my purpose is to illustrate the pluralism of Christianity, which necessarily reaches into the broader spectrum of other traditions represented in the world's most pluralistic polity. I also stress the style of engaging the policy process, not the specific substantive positions taken.

Two "Classical" Voices: Reinhold Niebuhr and John XXIII

The first example—perhaps *the* classical witness at the intersection of religion and foreign policy—is Reinhold Niebuhr (1892–1970), whose career reached from a Detroit Lutheran parish to three decades at Union Theological Seminary, a place from which he spoke to the church and the nation. No other single figure had Niebuhr's influence as a religious voice in the arena of foreign policy. In the 1960s, McGeorge Bundy called Niebuhr "probably the single most influential mind in the development of American attitudes which combine moral purpose with a sense of political reality."[10] A combination of factors accounted for Niebuhr's unique influence. He joined an ancient tradition of theological reflection with a powerfully incisive political mind; along with these personal gifts, he spoke from within the center of American Protestantism when it clearly dominated the American religious landscape. Niebuhr spoke for Protestantism, and he spoke for himself—he was a singular figure with the freedom to address issues across the spectrum of American public life. He commanded attention in the church, the American academy, and the popular media. Moreover, he was at the height of his personal capacities at the precise time when his scholarship fit the needs of U.S. foreign policy. Stanley Hoffmann's comment on the rise of the discipline of international relations in the United States (particularly the origins of political realism) applies analogously to Niebuhr's contribution:

> What the scholars offered, the policy-makers wanted. Indeed, there is a remarkable chronological convergence between their needs and the scholars' performances. Let us oversimplify greatly. What the leaders looked for, once the cold war started, was some intellectual compass which would serve multiple functions: exorcise isolationism, and justify a permanent and global involvement in world affairs; rationalize the accumulation of power, the techniques of intervention, and the methods of containment apparently required by the cold war; explain to a public of idealists why international politics does not leave much leeway for pure good will, and indeed besmirches purity; appease the frustrations of the bellicose by showing why unlimited force or extremism on behalf of liberty was no virtue; and reassure a nation eager for ultimate accommodation, about the possibility of both avoiding war and achieving its ideals. "Realism," however critical of specific policies, however (and thus self-contradictorily) diverse in its recommendations, precisely provided what was necessary.[11]

Niebuhr had already made a decisive contribution to the intersection of religion and foreign policy at the outset of World War II by creating a counterpoint to traditional Protestant pacifism with his moral defense of America's entry into the war. But the postwar setting provided him with an arena in which he became a national figure, waited upon by the intellectual and policy elites alike.[12]

Neibuhr's style of joining moral-religious vision with political complexity involved a number of sources woven together in a unique mix. He was a classical Protestant thinker in his abiding dependence on and explicit use of the Bible. The biblical categories were in turn developed with the help of Augustine's powerful sense that sin was a pervasive part of history and manifested itself in the aggressive behavior that is the stuff of world politics. A world scarred by sin required, as Augustine asserted and Niebuhr believed, the possible use of coercion, even to the point of war itself. War was not the principal theme in Niebuhr's political ethic. His fundamental concern was an understanding of power. Power was intrinsic to politics, and power needed both legitimation and limits. The fit between Niebuhr (and other versions of realism) and U.S. foreign policy in the early years of the cold war was the way in which they provided a rationale for a qualitatively new American engagement in world politics. Because of his cultural and religious influence Niebuhr's support for the postwar role of the United States had a resonance beyond that of other realists who actually had a more direct impact on the specific choices made in U.S. policy. But Niebuhr's distance from the intricacies of the policy process also gave him the space to play a more differentiated role than his realist colleagues. Niebuhr was not a stable ally for either church or state. He criticized the church when it failed to understand power and its necessity to achieve justice, and he criticized the state when it used power without legitimate reasons.

Niebuhr is often associated with other "realists" like George Kennan and Hans Morgenthau, all of whom had criticized customary American assumptions about foreign policy. Niebuhr did not have a singular identifiable impact on U.S. policy in the style of Kennan's "containment" doctrine or Morgenthau's status as the patriarch of international relations theory. Niebuhr's biographer, Richard Fox, describes Niebuhr's influence as participating with other key voices "in a system of influence in which some individuals and agencies established themselves as authoritative voices."[13] Niebuhr's authority with "insiders" like Kennan resided in his conception of the forces at work in human nature and human history. Arthur M. Schlesinger Jr. recalls Niebuhr's influence as a corrective to the liberal premise of regarding "human nature as benign and human society as perfectible."

But nothing in the system of human perfectibility had prepared us for Hitler and Stalin. The concentration camps and the gulags were proving human nature capable of infinite depravity. Niebuhr's interpretation of man and history came as a vast illumination.[14]

Fox notes that Niebuhr's political judgments were often not regarded as uniquely insightful. Nonetheless the philosophical-theological perspective that Kennan and Morgenthau valued yielded in Niebuhr's columns and articles a stream of commentary on communism, the future of Germany, the role of Europe, NATO and atomic weapons, and on through the gamut of foreign policy issues. These judgments certainly shaped the thought and views of many in the Protestant community who perhaps were more acquainted with the theological premises and needed more help with how premises led to particular conclusions. It is not possible to explore these conclusions here. It is best simply to cite Schlesinger's evaluation of Niebuhr's influence: "No man has had as much influence as a preacher in this generation; no preacher has had as much influence in the secular world."[15]

Niebuhr had no peer in the American religious community in the 1940s and 1950s. He was respected even by those who disagreed profoundly with his theological approach. This description fits perfectly the American Jesuit John Courtney Murray. At the very time Schlesinger was commending Niebuhr's vision of men and history, Murray wrote in *We Hold These Truths* a relentless critique of both; in Murray's view, Niebuhr's desire to address the complexity of human nature and the world of foreign policy led not to insight but to confusion. Murray did not disagree with many of Niebuhr's policy conclusions, but he represented an entirely different style of moral analysis, rooted in a different theological tradition.

> The real issue does not concern the moral quality of this or that element of American foreign policy. The real issue concerns the nature of morality itself, the determinants of moral action (whether individual or collective), the structure of the moral act, and the general style of moral argument.[16]

Murray was representing a tradition that Niebuhr had rejected as he found his way to Christian realism. The rejected moral vision was the classical natural law theory, rooted in pre-Christian authors but sustained in the Catholic tradition, not least by Murray himself. This analysis was philosophical in contrast to Niebuhr's theological perspective; it was confident of reason's capacity for drawing precise judgment in complex situations. Niebuhr found this confidence rationalistic, not sensitive to humanity's flawed nature and inclination to rationalize one's own self-interest.

Niebuhr and Murray engaged each other in the 1950s. In 1963 Pope John XXIII's encyclical, *Peace on Earth*, exemplified the tradition Murray defended and Niebuhr doubted in its assessment of global politics at the height of the cold war. Precisely because it was a papal text, it was bound to have less direct applicability to the U.S. foreign policy debate than a voice from within the country. But it was a voice of unique authority for a major religious community in the United States. The pope had determined to write *Peace on Earth* after the harrowing experience of the Cuban missile crisis in 1962. The document was published just before John XXIII died in May 1963, and it evoked a broad range of responses, from a commencement address by President John F. Kennedy to an article by Murray and a sympathetic but critical commentary by Niebuhr.

John XXIII addressed three broad topics in the papal letter: human rights, nuclear weapons, and the role of the United Nations.[17] In each case John XXIII moved the Catholic position forward: endorsing the concept of human rights with new clarity and systematization, casting doubt on any possible use of nuclear weapons, and arguing for a greater role of international institutions in world politics. These were notable positions for the Catholic community to hear in a teaching document, and they provided a new basis from which Catholics could engage the foreign policy debate in the United States. Only three years earlier Murray had lamented, "There seems, in fact, to be some reason for saying that the Catholic community is not much interested in foreign affairs, beyond its contribution in sustaining the domestic mood of anti-communism."[18]

In another context, it could be demonstrated that the combined effect of *Peace on Earth* and the impact of Vatican II did produce a changed posture of American Catholicism over the next twenty years on issues of foreign policy. The importance of *Peace on Earth* however, lies less in its policy conclusions and more in its style of analysis. To the question, how do distinct traditions develop a normative analysis of foreign policy issues, *Peace on Earth's* answer is strikingly different from a Niebuhrian Christian realism. The most evident difference is lack of reliance on and use of biblical resources. Niebuhr's arguments hardly ever moved far from a solid biblical foundation. *Peace on Earth* is almost entirely a philosophical analysis of the problem of order (moral and political) in world politics. In contrast to Niebuhr's thoroughly dialectical analysis of the complexity of policy issues, *Peace on Earth* develops the concept of order from the interpersonal to the international level in a seamless architecture of interlocking rights and duties.

Niebuhr's critique of the text questioned John XXIII's sense of how the national and international common good would be complementary most of the time. Throughout the letter Niebuhr worried about its "natural law optimism," its confidence that a shared moral vision could be sustained in the world community, and a reciprocal sense of shared interests developed. While Murray supported the moral theory of the letter, he too had reservations about its reading of the forces at work in the cold war.[19]

The tradition *Peace on Earth* represented still sustains a variety of authors, analysts, and policy advocates in the American community today. It offers a different moral lens than the one proffered by Niebuhr. But importantly both Christian realism and natural law have come under review and critique since the 1960s. Both have lost some of their traditional adherents, yet both have found, in the post–cold war era, new advocates. In that sense they remain part of our normative conversation on foreign policy. Significantly, Niebuhr's last book included a review and partial revision of his understanding of natural law, finding it more viable as a perspective on world affairs than he once thought.[20] There are contemporary analysts (I would be included) who find promise in drawing on these two traditions to address questions that neither Niebuhr nor John XXIII ever faced.

Contemporary Voices: Filling Out the Spectrum

Murray and Niebuhr worked in a religious setting much simpler in structure and scope than the United States is today. Both the Christian community and the wider religious world now have effective advocates who cannot be contained in the framework of Christian realism or Catholic natural law ethics. The effort here is simply to identify these voices without an attempt to analyze their contributions in any detail.

Remaining within the Christian community, the significant addition is the voice of evangelical Christians. This rapidly growing sector of the Christian community does not speak with one voice theologically or politically. Many years ago, when evangelical churches were gaining initial visibility in public policy debates, Max Stackhouse warned against unidimensional interpretations of who evangelicals were in the United States. He distinguished three strands of a broad Protestant movement: puritan, pietistic, and fundamentalist evangelicals.[21] Each had the capacity to produce a public agenda, and they could not simply be described as inevitably conservative in their positions. The popular phrase "religious right" applies only to some evangelicals.

Whether conservative or liberal in their conclusions, evangelicals are biblical in their premises. Their contribution to policy discourse invokes and uses the scriptures in a fashion distinct from Niebuhr and demonstrably different from the philosophical style of Murray or *Peace on Earth*.

Though evangelical positions are diverse, it is not a distortion to focus on the most visible and vocal group—evangelical Christians—who have provided strong support for conservative foreign policy positions. William Martin identifies their impact:

> the so-called Christian Right have put the United States, and indeed the rest of the world, on notice that religious conservatives will not limit their agenda to the water's edge. They are actively and increasingly involved in efforts to influence a wide range of U.S. policies, including support for Israel, arms control and defense and funding for the International Monetary Fund (IMF) and the United Nations.[22]

These issues are certainly not unique to the "Christian right." Other religious groups differ significantly in their conclusions but address a similar range of topics. Moreover, conservative evangelicals have convergent positions with other religious communities whose theological style is quite different. At times their opposition to abortion in population policy intersects with Catholic positions derived from a philosophical argument;

at other times voices in the "Christian right" are strong supporters of Israel. These alliances, however, have an ad hoc character about them, and they are not rooted deeply in a common style of moral analysis or a common style of advocacy.

Beyond the Christian community lie Judaism and Islam, both with solid core constituencies in the United States today. Jewish analysis and advocacy has been a consistent voice in modern American policy debates. Islam brings a theological-juridical tradition of policy ethics that is a recent contribution to foreign policy debates. Neither of these two ancient traditions is limited to issues of the Middle East, although both are vitally involved in any debate touching that region.

The proposition argued above in this article, that is, the changed perception of the significance of religion in world politics, creates new space and gives new weight to these diverse religious traditions that find a home in the United States. No tradition, nor any representative of a tradition, has the capacity to translate religious convictions or even moral principles directly into the policy process. Leo Ribuffo makes two complementary judgments that insightfully locate the role of religious reasoning: "no major diplomatic decision has turned on religious issues alone"; and "serious religious ideas have had at most an indirect impact on policymakers."[23] The modesty of these observations, however, should not eclipse the fact that the opportunity today to use an indirect impact effectively is a significant one.

Toward a Coherent Theory of Intervention

My response to the question of what moral direction a religious tradition can provide for U.S. policy regarding military intervention is anchored in the tradition that encompasses both the human rights perspective of *Peace on Earth* and the just war ethic. It is also the product of writing over the past ten years about adapting the just war ethic to a just intervention position.

Intervention covers a broad spectrum of actions; military intervention is the extreme case and the one that catalyzes the most debate politically and morally. Military intervention has also been a pervasive aspect of world politics. During the cold war, the two superpowers intervened within their defined spheres of influence without restraint (for example,

Hungary and Czechoslovakia; Guatemala and the Dominican Republic). They also intervened in countries where they believed even minor changes in the global balance of power could occur (Vietnam, Afghanistan); finally, they approached outright conflict in decisive areas of the world (Berlin, the Middle East) but kept their competition within specific boundaries.

This kind of "Great Power intervention" was a very different phenomenon than the issues the 1990s posed for humanitarian military intervention. No one pretended that either of the superpowers was moved by humanitarian intentions; both were catalyzed by conceptions of vital interests, even when many thought that these conceptions were politically misguided. Neither vital interest nor superpower competition was at stake in the choices of the 1990s; indeed it was the absence of both that shaped policy choices in that decade. Now in the first decade of a new century the policy choices differ from ones faced both during the cold war era and in the debates about humanitarian military intervention. Therefore, it may be useful to engage the present problems according to their location in a three-phase evolution of the political-moral argument about the place of intervention in world politics.[24]

First, the political-moral baseline for the argument is a well-known marker in the history of diplomacy. Rooted in the seventeenth century (part of the Westphalian synthesis), it was securely in possession before the founding of the United Nations but has been held less securely since then. The norm prohibited intervention by states in the domestic or internal jurisdiction of other sovereign states. The impetus for this rule had religious dimensions. It was created, as the earlier Kissinger quote noted, to restrain the pattern of universal intervention of the religious wars in Europe. From that original incentive the rule of nonintervention took on broader significance in world politics. It simultaneously reduced the reasons for the interstate conflict, helped to provide space for self-determination, and created a fragile but valuable barrier against interference in small states.[25] The multiple functions of the rule produced many advocates for its retention. But it also had its critics. The dark side was that it purchased interstate order at the price of ignoring intrastate violence and injustice.

The foundational documents of the United Nations paradoxically reaffirmed the rule of nonintervention and put in place a mortal threat to its viability. The opening paragraphs of the UN Charter constitute a clear, unequivocal endorsement of both the rights of sovereign states, and the requirement of all members, and the United Nations itself, to respect the domestic jurisdiction of states. Beyond the text of the charter, the United Nations produced two documents that embodied the challenge to the rule of nonintervention. The first, the Genocide Convention (1948), was as much a product of World War II as the charter itself. It sought to establish a clear limit to the restraint imposed by nonintervention; the existence of genocide called other states to take action. The second, a text of less legal significance than either the charter or a treaty, was the UN Declaration on Human Rights (1948). The essence of this document was precisely to establish standards against which the "internal order" of states was to be evaluated and the responsibility of states and international organizations for violations of human rights was affirmed. Neither of these documents had immediate impact on the inherited nonintervention rule, but together they contributed over time to the erosion of the absolute character of both sovereignty and nonintervention.

The moral tradition of the just war ethic, however, cannot simply be identified with the political-legal rule of nonintervention. The moral tradition, especially in its Christian context but not exclusively so, is grounded in a conviction about the unity of the human family. This conviction is a pervasive dimension of *Peace on Earth*. It yields, in turn, a fabric of duties and responsibilities for states that runs well beyond the inherited assumptions of the nonintervention rule. These duties of states required intervention on moral grounds even if legal support for such action was lacking. This fact became evident in the debates of the 1990s.

Indeed one way to characterize the second stage of the narrative on military intervention is to see the cases of the 1990s as examples of a crisis in international jurisprudence. The moral arguments made to support military action ran counter to the political-legal statutes of the nonintervention rule.[26] The cases that brought this jurisprudential conflict into the open ran through the decade of the 1990s: Bosnia, Haiti, East Timor, and Kosovo. The policy challenge they posed for states and international institutions is summarized in the report of the International Commission on Intervention and State Sovereignty:

External military intervention for human protection purposes has been controversial both when it has happened—as in Somalia, Bosnia and Kosovo—and when it has failed to happen, as in Rwanda. For some the new activism has been a long overdue internationalization of the human conscience; for others it has been an alarming breach of an international state order dependent on the sovereignty of states and the inviolability of their territory. For some, again, the only real issue is ensuring that coercive interventions are effective; for others, questions about legality, process and the possible misuse of precedent loom much larger.[27]

An effective response to this policy challenge requires two elements: a normative argument capable of winning broad support in the international community and a strategy that can be decisively implemented. Neither element was satisfactorily developed in the 1990s, but multiple efforts were made on both fronts. Normatively the most detailed proposals arose from several authors seeking to adapt "just war" to "just intervention." Although there were differences among several of us involved in this effort, we did agree on the broad outlines of a position. First, the nonintervention rule serves an essential function in an "anarchic" international system; hence the rule has a presumptive priority in addressing the decision on whether to intervene. Second, legitimation of intervention will, therefore, be restricted to a precisely defined set of cases. These cases must pass a version of the "just cause" test of the traditional ethic. Imposing this test illustrates that the moral argument is not meant to overturn the nonintervention rule but to limit the scope of its applicability. The just cause test will establish standards when the nonintervention presumption can be overridden by the moral duty of states "to rescue" or "to protect" individuals from rampant evil or domestic chaos.[28] Third, the "just cause" standard produced some cases for which intervention was agreed on: genocide, ethnic cleansing, and failed states.

In some cases authors and commentators were divided on the duty to rescue or protect, often focusing on how extensive human rights violations had to be to merit military intervention. Broad agreement existed that human rights violations demanded a range of political, legal, and economic responses, but military force was seen as a qualitatively different response. Fourth, a more controverted standard was the "proper authority" category of the just war ethic. Some authors give this category priority over all others in the just war tradition, but in the debate about intervention it divided analysts who could agree on cause to act but differed on who possessed the legitimate right to override nonintervention. Some held tightly to the Security Council as the sole and ultimate authority; others were willing to grant the right to regional organizations, or, more controversially, to alliances, or, finally, in extreme cases of necessity to any state that could effectively prevent harm. All found UN authorization desirable; not all were willing to let the absence of UN legitimation lead to paralysis.

Beyond these key tests even more pluralism could be found on judgments of "last resort" and "proportionality." Both were dependent on assessments of empirical data, and they were particularly difficult to invoke because the speed and fury of some of the internal conflicts (Rwanda uniquely) meant that hesitation could defeat the entire enterprise of rescue. Finally, all interventions are tested by the "just means" principles, both during the military operation and retrospectively, because a learning curve has developed over time about the ways to use limited force in these engagements, which always involve civilians in the midst of combat.

The 1990s did not produce a sufficiently strong and universally supported case to overturn the inherited political-legal standard of nonintervention. But the cumulative effect of arguments in the United Nations, among international lawyers and political scientists, and in the policy process of states moved the rule toward a recasting by the end of the decade. This yet unfinished argument was driven by the moral critique of nonintervention. The moral critique was not solely the product of a religious tradition, but it drew on premises and principles embodied in the just war view of how international relations should be understood. This summary is my effort to describe a wider process, but it is not uniquely mine nor solely the product of just war analysis; it does illustrate, however, how a religious tradition can be used to shape a broader secular case.

The unfinished arguments of the 1990s were not sufficient to confront the issues raised by the first decade of a new century. The terrorist attacks of September 11, 2001, followed by the interventions in Afghanistan and

Iraq, opened a plethora of arguments that were neither the issues of the cold war nor the choices about humanitarian intervention. A coherent theory of intervention must, however, relate the original baseline of non-intervention to the questions of the 1990s and the issues being raised, particularly by the United States, as it pursues the war on terrorism. Some question whether "war" is the appropriate organizing category for defining what the long-term response to terrorism will require.[29] But the attacks of 9/11 were consensually judged to legitimize a U.S. response invoking article 51 of the UN Charter. The U.S. intervention in Afghanistan, targeting the government and the al Qaeda organization, drew widespread support. It was intervention in response to a prior attack, and just war categories could be invoked directly to support the cause and the authority to act.

The more complex and controverted issues arose when the response to terror extended beyond Afghanistan to other countries (Yemen, Philippines, Indonesia) and, most important, to Iraq. The debate about Iraq clearly went beyond the arguments of the 1990s, and it raised some of the older questions about Great Power intervention. Iraq was clearly not about humanitarianism (even though Hussein's human rights record was reprehensible in scope and savagery); it was also not a linear case about terrorism, since the links existing with al Qaeda were a matter of much dispute. The U.S. case for war was a mix of several reasons: that Iraq possessed some and sought to produce other weapons of mass destruction (WMD), that UN authorization existed to enforce resolutions from the early 1990s, that regime change was necessary to solve the first two problems, that the Iraqi people deserved to be rescued from the grip of a malicious regime. Unlike 1991, however, there was not a clear case of international aggression that could galvanize an international response, particularly in the Security Council. The proposed action against Iraq was, therefore, unauthorized military intervention. In addition, the appearance in September 2002 of an official policy paper of the U.S. government, *The National Security Strategy of the United States*, made it clear that the reasoning being used to support intervention in Iraq could be extended to other countries.[30] Hence the Iraq debate was two dimensional: Was intervention justified, and would it set a precedent for other military actions? The U.S. case was pressed on the basis that the world faced a new and different kind of threat, certainly not the kind posed by humanitarian crises but also not the kind envisioned by those who had shaped the traditional nonintervention rule.

The new threat was defined as the combination of "radicalism and technology" or the existence of WMD and terrorist groups in search of such weapons. The link between the two terms was states possessing WMD that were "rogue states" (a Clinton-era term) willing to defy nonproliferation norms and willing to aid terrorism. In the face of this triad the U.S. case implied or asserted that traditional norms of statecraft, diplomacy, and international law had to be revised. The revisions would be far reaching. Intervention would be justified for political-strategic reasons even if aggression had not occurred; the second war against Iraq would not rely on the rationale of the Gulf War. Moreover, the United States asserted the right to act unilaterally to defeat the mix of "radicalism and technology"; this posed a severe challenge to the basic principles of the UN Charter. Finally, law and practice would have to be reinterpreted to accommodate preemptive military action—actually preventive war—because classical concepts of deterrence would not work in this new environment. Henry Kissinger, writing in support of the administration's policy, captured its far-reaching character: "The new approach is revolutionary . . . the notion of justified preemption runs counter to modern international law, which sanctions the use of force in self-defense against actual, not potential, threats."[31]

The U.S.-led military intervention in Iraq to depose Saddam Hussein and disarm Iraq of WMD employed all of these proposed revisions of law and politics. Undertaken without Security Council legitimation and with a divided NATO alliance, the successful prosecution of the war opens the question of whether the action sets a precedent for other cases and for other states to follow. Some of the supporters of U.S. policy challenged those who had argued for humanitarian interventions in the 1990s to see the Iraq case as equally legitimate.[32] But this linear extension is not self-evidently necessary or even desirable from a moral perspective.

Rather than simply sweep the Iraq case into the framework of the 1990s debate, a coherent theory of intervention will have to address independently each stage of the narrative sketched in this essay. The Iraq case resembled much more the Great Power interventions of the eighteenth and nineteenth centuries (and to some degree the cold war) than it did any of the interventions of the 1990s. To be sure there were humanitarian dimensions to it because of the virtually universal condemnation of Saddam Hussein's regime. But it was not driven by humanitarian motives or causes. What did drive it was a combination of traditional vital interest arguments joined with some authentically new characteristics of the post-9/11 world.

A coherent theory of intervention should begin with the argument that the traditional baseline nonintervention rule, stated without exceptions or qualifications, cannot stand today. To save it (which we should for moral, legal, and political reasons) we will have to revise it. The process should continue with a description of the multiple forms of intervention in world politics today. The process of globalization, built on the increased interdependence of states, has significantly multiplied the possibilities for state and nonstate actors to be agents of intervention in the lives of others. Next, there should be a political-moral argument made separating military intervention from other examples; this analysis would draw on the just war ethic's classification of force as the *ultima ratio*, the very last instrumentality to be engaged in relationships among states. The political-moral rationale for the classification needs to be set forth because it will provide the basis for later restrictions to be placed on the use of force.

The next step would be to distinguish clearly and precisely that there are different kinds of military intervention, each requiring a different mode of justification. Revising the baseline rule of nonintervention means providing specific justification to override the rule. I believe this has been going on in the case of humanitarian military intervention. In a critical mass of analysis, generally based on just war categories, a convincing critique of the baseline rule of nonintervention has been developed. If September 11 had not occurred, a definitive rewriting of the rule could have been carried off. That prospect awaits renewed attention.

In contrast, there are few voices who seek a return to an imperial world where intervention is simply a prerogative of a Great Power. But there are two kinds of intervention now being advocated that go beyond humanitarian intervention; in my view they threaten to erode the fundamental role that the nonintervention rule plays in world politics. In making a case against these two proposals, it is necessary to acknowledge that they emerge from the same logic that produced the revisions on humanitarian intervention—the logic of defining exceptions to a generally valid rule.

The first proposal is to justify the use of military force to rectify persistent human rights violations. The debates of the 1990s led to a conclusion that genocide as the sole exception to nonintervention was not an adequate moral framework. Ethnic cleansing, for example, may not reach the level of genocide, but the experience of Bosnia led many, correctly I believe, to legitimate military action to prevent ethnic cleansing. In 2003, there are advocates of using military power in the cause of human rights and democratization. But a linear extension of military intervention for these two valid objectives could produce open-ended intervention. An unqualified standard of human rights violations as a trigger for the use of force might well have supported such interventions across Latin America in the 1970s. Faced with this possibility, the "proportionality" category of the just intervention ethic leads me to conclude that the just cause argument is being extended too broadly in these human rights cases. Moreover, the complexity of institutionalizing democracy in diverse political and cultural systems gives even greater weight to a proportionality test that *could justify* a human rights policy (using a mix of carrots and sticks) but not *military* intervention.

The harder case is the second proposal: using force to prevent or reverse proliferation of weapons of mass destruction. This case, which was a major theme in the George W. Bush administration's argument that war with Iraq was necessary, raises the question of whether the entire policy governing nonproliferation should be rethought in light of 9/11. The policy in place since the 1970s has been a diplomatic initiative. It divided the world into nuclear and nonnuclear states and sought to prevent proliferation through persuasion, the promise of benefits, and the threat of sanctions. The possible use of military action was never denied, but it was never at the forefront of the policy. The Clinton administration's endorsement of counterproliferation signaled a change in U.S. posture, and the "national security strategy" moves in the direction of legitimizing preventive war.

The arguments used to support this substantial shift of policy are that deterrence at best is partially effective today; that distinctions have to be drawn between different kinds of possessing states (India and Pakistan versus Iraq and North Korea); and that terrorist networks seeking WMD make preventive war a necessary option for the United States to have available. This proposal, to include preventive war in the list of justifiable interventions, is quite unlike comparing different kinds of human rights violations. Is the threat or the fact of proliferation a just cause for intervention? Does it matter whether the state to be attacked had entered a legal agreement not to proliferate? What constitutes the trigger for intervention? Is it the threat of proliferation, the possession of WMD, threats made against other states? Is it the record of the proliferating state?

In my view a coherent theory of intervention cannot rule out absolutely intervention to address threats to the international system (and specific states) posed by WMD, but all the questions I just raised would have to be verified before just cause could be affirmed. Moreover, cause by itself would not suffice; this is Great Power intervention, the very kind the original rule of nonintervention was designed to prevent; the authority of a single state to act is not sufficient (unless article 51 applies). If proliferation is a systemic threat, one with consequences for more than a state or a region, then systemic legitimation through the Security Council is needed for preventive war. The Bush administration acknowledged that revision of international law would likely be needed to justify the policy it was advocating.[33]

Beyond cause and legitimation the relevant means test should be limited to conventional weapons. First use of nuclear weapons in a preventive war strategy should not be legitimated; the nature of the weapons and the provocative character of a preemption-prevention strategy are reasons to rule out this declaratory or use policy.

These criteria provide a marginal possibility for justified intervention to address WMD. Their purpose is to make the case only marginal at best. This grudging acknowledgment of some possible legitimation flows from the conviction that the proposed doctrine of preemption and preventive war tilts international relations in the wrong direction, toward more frequent uses of force by many states.

The complexity of this one topic (military intervention), which is only one of several that could have been used to illustrate the intersection of moral, religious, and political forces at work in the post-9/11 world, demonstrates the potential of these arguments in understanding and seeking to shape (even if only indirectly) U.S. foreign policy in a new and dangerous era.

Notes

1. Michael Doyle, "Ethics and International Relations: A Speculative Essay," in Anthony Lake and David Ochmanek, eds., *The Real and the Ideal* (Rowman and Littlefield Publishers, Inc., 2002), p. 47.

2. The story of how previous conceptions of world politics and foreign policy are being brought under review and revision has been narrated by many authors. I seek only to summarize the story here because it poses the background for our discussion in this volume. An excellent summary is Daniel Philpott, "The Challenge of September 11 to Secularism in International Relations," *World Politics,* vol. 55 (October 2002), pp. 66–95.

3. Ibid., p. 71.

4. Henry A. Kissinger, *Does America Need a Foreign Policy?* (Simon and Schuster, 2001), p. 236.

5. The assessment of sovereignty—its continuing significance and new limits—cuts across every major discussion in world politics. Examples include Stanley Hoffmann, "The Clash of Globalizations," *Foreign Affairs,* vol. 81 (July–August 2002), pp. 104–15; a catalyst for analysis has been Robert O. Keohane and Joseph S. Nye, *Power and Interdependence* (Little, Brown, 1977), pp. 3–37.

6. Kissinger, *Does America Need a Foreign Policy?*, p. 234.

7. Ibid., p. 235.

8. J. Bryan Hehir, "The Uses of Force in the Post–Cold War World," Working Paper (Washington: Woodrow Wilson International Center, 1996), p. 9.

9. Leo P. Ribuffo, "Religion in the History of U.S. Foreign Policy," in Elliott Abrams, ed., *The Influence of Faith: Religious Groups and U.S. Foreign Policy* (Rowman and Littlefield, 2001), pp. 1–30.

10. McGeorge Bundy, "Foreign Policy: From Innocence to Engagement," in Arthur M. Schlesinger Jr. and Morton White, eds., *Paths of American Thought* (Boston, 1963), cited in Richard W. Fox, *Reinhold Niebuhr: A Biography* (Pantheon Books, 1985), p. 276.

11. Stanley Hoffmann, "An American Social Science: International Relations," in *Janus and Minerva: Essays in the Theory and Practice of International Politics* (Westview Press, 1987), p. 10.

12. Fox, *Reinhold Niebuhr*, chaps. 9–11.

13. Ibid., p. 239.

14. Arthur M. Schlesinger Jr., *A Life in the Twentieth Century: Innocent Beginnings, 1917–1950* (Houghton-Mifflin, 2000) p. 250.

15. Arthur M. Schlesinger Jr., "Reinhold Niebuhr's Role in American Political Thought and Life," in Charles Kegley and Robert W. Bretall, eds., *Reinhold Niebuhr: His Religious, Social and Political Thought* (Macmillan Co., 1956), p. 149.

16. John Courtney Murray, *We Hold These Truths: Catholic Reflections on the American Proposition* (Sheed and Ward, 1960), p. 282.

17. John XXIII, *Peace on Earth*, in Thomas Shannon and David O'Brien, eds., *Catholic Social Thought: The Documentary Heritage* (Orbis Books, 1992), pp. 131–62.

18. Murray, *We Hold These Truths*, p. 291.

19. John Courtney Murray, *Things Old and New in* Pacem in Terris, in J. Leon Hooper, ed., *Bridging the Sacred and the Secular: Selected Writings of John Courtney Murray, S.J.* (Georgetown University Press, 1994), pp. 252–53.

20. Reinhold Niebuhr, *Man's Nature and His Communities* (Charles Scribner's Sons, 1965).

21. Max Stackhouse, "Religious Right: New? Right?" *Commonweal* (January 29, 1982), p. 53.

22. William Martin, "The Christian Right and American Foreign Policy," *Foreign Policy*, vol. 114 (Spring 1999), p. 67.

23. Ribuffo, "Religion in the History of U.S. Foreign Policy," p. 21.

24. For an overview of the problem see Stanley Hoffmann, "The Politics and Ethics of Military Intervention," *Survival*, vol. 37 (1995–96), pp. 29–51.

25. J. Bryan Hehir, "Sovereignty and Nonintervention: Recasting the Relationship," in Jonathan Moore, ed., *Hard Choices: Moral Dilemmas in Humanitarian Intervention* (Rowman and Littlefield, 1998), p. 40.

26. Catherine Guicherd, "International Law and the War in Kosovo," *Survival*, vol. 41 (Summer 1999), pp. 19–34.

27. Report of the International Commission on Intervention and State Sovereignty, *The Responsibility to Protect* (Ottawa, Canada: International Development Research Center, 2001), p. vii.

28. Ibid.; and see also *Social Research*, vol. 62 (Spring 1995).

29. Michael Howard, "What's in a Name?" *Foreign Affairs*, vol. 81 (January–February 2002), p. 9.

30. *The National Security Strategy of the United States of America*, White House, Washington D.C. (September 2002).

31. Henry A. Kissinger, "Our Intervention in Iraq," *Washington Post*, August 12, 2002, p. A15.

32. Robert Kagan, "War and the Fickle Left," *Washington Post*, December 24, 2002, p. A15.

33. *The National Security Strategy*, p. 15.

CAN THERE BE A
MORAL FOREIGN POLICY?

MICHAEL WALZER

W HEN I SAW the topic originally proposed for this discussion, "faith, morals, and foreign policy," I decided immediately that I would talk mostly about morals, not about faith, which is perhaps a Jewish strategy for dealing with these matters.

Faith has never played the role in Judaism that it plays in Christianity. But for Jews and Christians alike, and for just about everyone else too, religion has been a powerful force in shaping moral ideas and values, not only generally but also with specific reference to politics and war. For reasons that I describe below, these ideas about morality don't come glued to any particular religion; nor are they a function of actual belief, faith in the literal sense. In the contemporary world, I suggest that we need to worry about faith—for when it turns into dogma and certainty, as it frequently does, it tends to override morality. A faith-based foreign policy would be a very bad idea.

Against Realism

But does morality, even when it's not overridden, have anything at all to do with foreign policy? The claim of the people who call themselves "realists," who preen themselves as Machiavellian princes or as Machiavellian advisers to princes, is that morality never has to be overridden; from the beginning it is nothing more than a façade behind which states pursue their strategic interests. Political leaders seize the available opportunities, or they are driven by military necessity. When they are hard-pressed, they do what they have to do; in a position of strength, they do whatever they can. No doubt, that is often true—or it is true often enough so that "realism" isn't a crazy position. But I don't think that it is always true, and I want to suggest—provocatively, I hope, but also realistically—that sometimes the opposite is true: strategic arguments about what is possible or necessary are a façade behind which political and military leaders act out their deepest moral and political convictions.

One example illustrates my point: the debate about strategic bombing policy in Britain in the early years of World War II. The debate has been much written about, and its central focus is fairly well known.[1] Military strategists and political leaders argued about what the Royal Air Force, Britain's only effective weapon at that point in the war, should try to do. Should its goal be to kill as many German civilians as possible, so as to demoralize the enemy and shut down the economy, or should the planes aim only at military targets—railroad yards, tank factories, and army bases? The debate was conducted, as far as I can tell, entirely in the language of strategy. The idea that civilians were innocent men and women, immune from direct attack, was never mentioned. Instead, the questions posed were radically "realistic": What were the probabilities of hitting military targets, given the navigational and aiming devices then available? What losses would the air force suffer if it flew by day, or at lower altitudes, so as to aim (a little) more precisely? How would bombing urban residential areas affect civilian morale and the production and delivery of military supplies? Outside the British government a few people raised moral questions about bombing policy (the most memorable protest came from a Jesuit priest, John C. Ford, in an essay called "The Morality of Obliteration Bombing"[2]). Inside the government, there seemed to be a ban on moral talk: there's no one here but us realists! In the years after the war, however, the people who favored bombing residential areas turned out to be advisers and office-holders in Tory governments, and the people who opposed it were active on the left, working for Labor governments or for the Campaign for Nuclear Disarmament. For both these groups, it seems clear that their moral and political convictions—most crucially, their views about the rightness or wrongness of killing enemy civilians—had driven their wartime arguments. I suspect that something similar was true in this country in the run-up to the Iraq war. The conflicting intelligence estimates provided to the Bush administration (and to other governments too) seem to have been governed by the ideological commitments of the providers or tailored to fit the ideology of the recipients. After all, strategists commonly work from inadequate and uncertain information, and their predictions are cast in rough probabilities. They can easily go either way, and they seem to go, very often, the way the people making them want them to go.

It is a great mistake, then, to underestimate the importance of moral and political convictions. They are not the whole story. I don't mean to deny the force of self-interest or the value of cost-benefit analysis; the second of these figures later on in my argument. But it is important to insist now that morality has practical consequences.

Toward a More Moral Foreign Policy

My argument begins with four propositions for a more moral foreign policy.

The first obligation of the state, any state, is its Hobbesian obligation to protect the lives of its citizens. "Homeland security" is indeed what states are about, even though that phrase jars us a bit here in the United States, since we were taught to think of America as a promised land, not a homeland. And one of the things that is promised, perhaps the most important thing, is liberty—which has to be balanced against security and not set aside for security's sake. Protecting life and liberty together is the first obligation of our own state.

The second obligation is not to inflict harm on the citizens of other states. The point is obvious, but at the same time, the political and economic harms inflicted by U.S. policies, and by those of other states too, are manifold. Even when we act justly, we often put other people at risk, and we often harm them. And then the obligation is to repair the harm, as best we can. In international politics, reparation is far more important than repentance or apology.

The third obligation is to help citizens of other states, when it is possible to do so, to avoid or escape the crimes and disasters of collective life: genocide, tyranny, conquest, ethnic cleansing, famine, and pandemic disease. This is what philosophers call an "imperfect duty," since it is difficult to say exactly when we, rather than the British or the French, for example, or the Russians or the Chinese, ought to help this particular group of people in trouble. Given the extent of crimes and disasters in the contemporary world, how is the responsibility to help distributed among possible agents? There are no agreed-on distributional criteria, but it seems safe to say that the United States, because of its wealth and power and its sometime involvement in the crimes and disasters, has a significant share of the responsibility.

The fourth obligation is to help the citizens of other states, when they want to be helped, to build decent and nonrepressive political systems. This is another imperfect duty and, again, the responsibility of the United States looms large. But there are good reasons to think that this kind of help would come most effectively from international agencies like the United Nations or from the new nongovernmental organizations (NGOs) that constitute the international version of civil society. Within or alongside these organizations, individual states could play their larger and smaller parts.

These propositions can be expressed and understood in different cultural idioms. We can be guided in fulfilling the four obligations by a variety of moral traditions, both religious and secular in character. Some of the traditions, like those of the West, exist in religious and secular versions, and when this is so, the two versions are not far apart. Indeed, they should not differ at all according to standard Jewish and Christian teaching, since knowledge of the morality of social and political life does not depend on a historical revelation to a particular people or on faith in a particular creed. Catholic moral philosophy is an exposition of what are called "natural laws" because they are knowable to all of us; they follow from certain facts about our common human nature. The Jewish doctrine is similar: "These are the rational laws," says Judah Halevi in *The Kuzari*, "being the basis and preamble of divine law, preceding it in character and time, and being indispensable in the administration of human society. Even a gang of robbers [he is paraphrasing an argument from Plato's *Republic* here] must have a kind of justice among them if their confederacy is to last."[3] And what is true for the members of the robber gang is true for the rest of us: "God is equally gracious to all," as Spinoza wrote.

He meant that the laws of morality are universally available to human reason.[4]

I don't deny that these laws can be worked out in different ways and expressed in different idioms. I have always argued that they can be and are. But we recognize all the worked-out sets of laws as *moralities*. And the moral principles expressed in the different idioms overlap extensively with one another. We can describe this "overlapping consensus" in, let's say, Jewish, or Christian, or secular languages. And it obviously matters a great deal to individual men and women that they are allowed to speak in the language of their choice. But from a more distanced perspective, it doesn't matter much which language they choose, as long as the arguments and principles really overlap.

Just War Theory

Consider the example of just war theory, which can be taken as an expression of the laws of nature, a construction of reason, or even, perhaps, a modus vivendi for robber gangs. It regulates state behavior in regard to the first and third of my opening propositions, whenever these two require states to go to war, in self-defense or in defense of others. As a systematic theory, just war has its origin in Catholic moral philosophy.[5] But as a set of propositions about aggression, self-defense, humanitarian intervention, noncombatant immunity, the treatment of prisoners of war, and much else, it has a more complicated and diverse history. We might even say that it originates in many different places—in all the places, in fact, where wars have been fought. In any case, Catholic just war theory was incorporated into and adapted to the uses of international law in the seventeenth and eighteenth centuries, and it was rediscovered by secular moral philosophers and political theorists in the twentieth century. It is, I believe, triumphant today, having supplanted many alternative ways of talking about war.[6]

Perhaps "supplanted" is too strong a word. There is an alternative tradition, a medieval rival of just war, which has not been wholly supplanted: the crusade, the holy war, the jihad. All these words describe a faith-based struggle against the forces of darkness and evil, which are generally understood in explicitly religious terms: infidels, idolaters, the antichrist. In the

West, especially after 9/11, we are a little leery about holy wars, and so when President George W. Bush talks about war in religiously inflected terms, someone is sure to reprimand him, and his advisers will insist, possibly rightly, that he did not mean that we are actually engaged in a crusade on God's behalf. Nonetheless, there are some Americans, fundamentalist Protestants mostly, who see the world in exactly those terms. They claim a role for religion in shaping U.S. foreign policy that is not mediated by natural law or universal reason but rather by biblical literalism and dogmatic conviction. By contrast, just war is a mediated and secular doctrine and has been that pretty much from its beginnings. The classic statement of its secularism came in the early sixteenth century from the Spanish Dominican Francisco de Vitoria: "Difference of religion cannot be a cause of just war." And what is a just cause? Vitoria is equally specific. "The sole and only just cause for waging war is when harm has been inflicted."[7]

The just war arguments in which Americans are currently engaged—about self-defense and humanitarian intervention, about preemption and terrorism—are definitely focused on "harms inflicted" (or, in the case of preemption, on harms that are supposedly about to be inflicted). These arguments can be worked out in the language of Catholic natural law, or in the language of the international lawyers, or in the language of contemporary analytic philosophy. Each of these is probably translatable without much loss into the other, and so, again, it doesn't matter which one we choose to speak. There are differences, though, and so I should acknowledge that I speak here as a philosopher. But not an academic philosopher: the harms that we are talking about today, in the new age of mass murder and terrorism, require a political or military response, and so the moral arguments we make should be aimed at shaping the policies of our government.

Do the different versions of just war theory have, each of them, some characteristic weakness that doesn't appear in the others? Are there dangers in speaking "as a philosopher" or as a lawyer or a priest? The most important weaknesses, it seems to me, are common to all versions of the theory or, better, to all the theorists. They are human weaknesses: the tendency toward accommodation and rationalization, on the one hand, and the tendency toward absolutism, on the other. Right now, secular thinkers are probably more likely to display the first of these and religious thinkers the second, but these associations are temporary and uncertain. They don't reflect specific features of either secularism or religion.

These two tendencies are common in moral life generally. They are responses to the simple fact that any theory about justice will stand in tension with the existing patterns of political practice. That is not because, or not necessarily because, politicians are wicked or power hungry or selfishly opportunistic, though those descriptions fit many of the ones we know and love, but rather because politicians, even the best of them, operate in a world of conflicting interests and values. They are constantly forced into compromises that are, as we say, morally compromising. They do less than they know they should be doing, or they pretend to be doing more than they are doing, or they act badly in the hope that good will come, or they form alliances with bad people. Some theorists are much too eager to understand and excuse these compromises as "necessary" features of political life. And others are much too eager to condemn every one of them, without making any effort to understand their occasions. These are two ways of getting morally lost. In the first case, one is lost in the endless adjustments of principle to expedience; in the second, one is lost in the distant reaches of righteousness.

Humanitarian Intervention

What does it mean not to get lost, to sustain a critical engagement with the real world? I want to answer this question by joining the argument about humanitarian intervention. The obligation of capable states to protect endangered citizens of other states, the third of my posited obligations, is widely accepted today but rarely fulfilled. There are no differences among the different moral traditions or among the different versions of just war theory with regard to the wrongness of massacre and ethnic cleansing. But significant disagreements do exist—about who should intervene, when and how, under whose authority, and with what degree of force—not among traditions but within them. When Elie Wiesel urged President Bill Clinton to act forcefully in Bosnia, he spoke with an urgency motivated by the twentieth-century Jewish experience of disaster. But there was nothing peculiarly Jewish in his recognition that something awful was going on in Bosnia. And American Jews disagreed among themselves about who should act and how, as did American Catholics, even when they appealed to a theory of just war that they supposedly held in common.

Still, just war theory as I understand it does suggest some answers to the questions about who, when, and how. I offer them in the hope of winning agreement from the very large number of people who, theorists or not, believe that states ought to fight only when their cause is just and only when they can fight justly.[8]

First, in a system of sovereign states, multilateral action is preferable to the action of single states, since it protects those acted on from imperial ambition and state aggrandizement. But multilateralism is often ineffective in practice; it often isn't possible to get states to act together, even in the face of terrible humanitarian crises. And so unilateral military responses to crimes against humanity are defensible and sometimes morally necessary. The Vietnamese intervention to shut down the killing fields of Cambodia and the Tanzanian intervention to overthrow the regime of Idi Amin in Uganda are useful examples. Authorization by the United Nations is not a legitimacy requirement for humanitarian intervention (it wasn't even imaginable in Cambodia or Uganda). One might argue the reverse: the UN puts its legitimacy at risk when it fails to authorize military action in the face of terrible crimes.

Second, the inability to act in one case doesn't require a state, for the sake of moral consistency, to refuse to act in other cases. Prudential calculations may sometimes preclude intervention even in the face of crimes against humanity, but that fact can't be used to justify inaction in cases for which the same calculations produce a different result. The United Nations didn't have to stay out of East Timor, for example, just because it failed to intervene in Tibet. Consistency in such matters is, as Emerson wrote in "Self-Reliance," "the hobgoblin of little minds."[9]

Third, the likelihood, even the certainty, of civilian deaths is not a bar to military action that is necessary to stop massacre or ethnic cleansing—as long as positive steps are taken to minimize the number of civilians killed, and as long as the number is not disproportionate to the disaster that is averted. The doctrine of double effect developed by Catholic philosophers reflecting on the unintended consequences of our actions is still a good doctrine. I don't believe that it is best understood, however, as an argument about intentionality. It is an argument about what we ought to do when we know that we can't fully control the consequences of our actions. Once we recognize that the military campaign we are planning would impose risks on men and women who are not our enemies or our targets, we have to take measures to protect those people. It isn't enough "not to intend" that civilians get killed; we have to intend that they not get killed—and the only test of intention in cases like this is action. Grappling with the arguments about double effect is a useful example, one of the best possible examples, of what critical engagement with the real world requires.

When we engage in this way, we have to resist the same two dangers that I have already discussed: absolutism and accommodation. To oppose military action in every case in which it might have deadly side effects— "collateral damage" is the current euphemism—is to fall into a bad utopianism. I have heard this opposition defended in recent years, but the defense doesn't seem to me politically or morally serious. It effectively turns just war theory into a form of pacifism. But if an absolute ban on war-making is the goal, surely there are more direct and forthright ways of reaching it. However, to justify all the deadly side effects without setting limits on their scope and on how they are produced is to accept what should never be accepted.

Finally, the notion that force is the last resort in any moral or political crisis is not a plausible guide to foreign policy decisionmaking. Military resistance may rightly be the first resort of a state or nation facing armed aggression—the Finns in 1939, say, confronting Russian invaders. The moral meaning of lastness is simply that whenever there are alternatives to the use of force, and time to try them out, we are morally bound to do that. But the timely use of force can be justified, even if there is still time to send another diplomatic note or call another meeting. In fact, there is always time to do something, or to do it again, before deciding on the use of force, but it isn't wise or right to refrain from forceful action against an aggression or massacre in progress on the grounds that we haven't yet reached the "last resort." There is a sense in which we never reach it or never can reach it. Lastness is a metaphysical condition, ultimately unreachable, whereas political action must be timely if it is to be effective.

Moral Traditions and Foreign Aid

I have been arguing that one can be critically engaged through the medium of different moral and religious traditions. I'm not inclined to insist, at least not now, on the value of any particular one. Indeed, it's possible to make arguments like the ones I have just been making about humanitarian intervention, without the support of any tradition—speaking, as it were, for oneself alone, in the language of pure reason. Still, political and moral criticism is stronger if the critics are able to argue within a common tradition of some sort, for then the concepts and categories they use will be widely known, and insofar as they use them persuasively, they will take on something of the authority of the tradition. They don't speak only for themselves but lay claim to the accumulated wisdom of many generations.

I stress that this is accumulated *human* wisdom. Even people who work within religious traditions should never lay claim to, should never be allowed to lay claim to, divine authority. That move is designed to silence opponents and critics; it is the discursive equivalent of crusading warfare. I leave aside the peculiar intensity, zeal, and remorselessness with which policies commanded by God are commonly carried out (since intensity, zeal, and remorselessness have also played a part in secular political movements). I mean to focus only on the use of God's name to stop the argument. A healthy tradition cannot tolerate stops of that sort. All claims are open to dispute. Traditions are sites for arguments, and that's not less true of religious than of secular traditions. They are useful sites, because the arguments that go on there are worth winning, even if the victories are almost always temporary. If I make a strong case, using commonly recognized concepts and categories, that this war is unjust, or that this humanitarian intervention is morally necessary, I have done something more than express an opinion. I have occupied the discursive high ground, as we all mean to do, and now the burden of the argument falls on anyone who wants to defend the war or oppose the intervention.

The usefulness of traditional argument is especially obvious when we have to challenge received opinion or vested interest. So consider another example of my third posited obligation, widely recognized and rarely fulfilled: the need to intervene to avoid or mitigate the effects of global poverty, famine, and pandemic disease. Given the extent of unnecessary pain and death in the world today, the argument for massive resource transfers from rich to poor countries can be made, exactly like the argument for humanitarian intervention, within any of the existing moral and religious traditions. Obviously, the transfers are not taking place—or their scope is tiny, given the need. But that is not (yet) evidence that the arguments are ineffective. Every wealthy or even merely prosperous government in the West and North has a very strong interest in minimizing the transfers. Indeed, it is probably harder to argue for massive resource transfers than for large-scale military interventions (but why is this so?). And yet, distributional issues are now on the global political agenda. Campaigns to lower the cost of therapeutic drugs in poor countries, or to alter the terms of trade, or to control financial speculation and capital flight are, all of them, morally driven, even if some of their protagonists also act for strategic or partisan reasons. None of these campaigns has produced anything more than small successes. But the critical attack on global inequality has only just begun.[10]

As it develops, critics will certainly explore the uses of traditional concepts and categories. They will appeal to conscience, which is to say to the moral knowledge that human beings share with God or one another, depending on how one views such matters. In any case, the idea of a common humanity is part of that shared knowledge, which can be expressed in religious terms (we are all created in the image of God) or in secular terms (we share the same rational capacity and physical vulnerability, we live in the same world of economic and political interdependence). I am not sure that we *understand* our obligations within the available moral or religious traditions. Moral understanding is a deep subject, and I cannot claim to know how we come to it. I suspect that the route is indirect. But we explain our obligations to one another within the traditions, and we argue about their extent and about exactly what actions they require, individually and collectively.

Let me suggest four sets of questions about global inequality and foreign aid that we need to address. Readers will have no difficulty recognizing concepts and categories that already figure in our moral consciousness.

First, to what extent have the prevailing inequalities been created by willful human action? Do they follow from a history of military conquest, colonial rule, economic exploitation, financial speculation, and other state, corporate, or entrepreneurial decisions, or are they largely the consequences of geography and culture? We can be bound in different ways to help poor and hungry people around the world, but we are bound most tightly if we are in some significant, even if partial, way responsible for their poverty and hunger.

Second, what sacrifices are we obligated to make in order to reduce the suffering of the world's poorest people? The easiest argument for global transfers is that a very small percentage of the GNP of the world's wealthiest nations would make an enormous difference in the everyday life of the most impoverished. That seems true, but what if, down the road, a more substantial percentage is required?

Three, how is the responsibility to act distributed among individuals and states? What should we be doing today and tomorrow, and with what other people should we be doing it?

Four, how should we in the wealthiest nations respond to the self-destructive politics, the corruption and violence, of many of the poorest countries? What should we do in cases of state failure, warlord tyranny, and ethnic wars? What kinds of political or economic pressure or intervention are permitted, if they are necessary, to make external assistance effective for the neediest people?

I cannot pretend to have the answers to these questions. Perhaps, indeed, they are too hard; perhaps the effort to respond is politically unproductive, and so the questions should be avoided whenever we can avoid them. Think back to America's first and most massive entry into the project of foreign aid, the Marshall Plan. My memory of the debates of the late 1940s—I was only on the brink of political consciousness at that time—is that the crucial argument in favor of helping European recovery was an argument from enlightened self-interest (clearly that is the only argument that would have appealed to Dean Acheson as he is described in Bryan Hehir's chapter). George Marshall and other leading figures in the Truman administration also made claims about political affinity and moral solidarity. I don't recall how the claims were cast—not, I suspect, in religious terms. Nor were the American people told that we were responsible for the desperate condition of Europe after World War II, because we didn't intervene to stop Hitler in the 1930s, say, or because our armies contributed to the devastation of the continent in the 1940s. The Marshall Plan was not driven by liberal guilt but rather by a lively sense of interdependence and common destiny. Europe and America were "in this together," however "this" was understood.

Half a century later, it's time to start thinking about the rest of the world in similar terms. Of course, we should address critical problems of famine and disease, the AIDS epidemic in Africa, the brutal exploitation of children in many parts of the Third World, the persecution of religious and ethnic minorities, and much else, in humanitarian terms, drawing on the moral traditions that explain our duties to fellow human beings who are strangers to us. But will the humanitarian arguments by themselves carry the day? What should we make of a success like the Marshall Plan, in which they played only a background role? I began this essay by arguing that moral ideas have real world consequences, but it is probably our negative morality that is most consequential in the world. "Don't kill civilians" is a strong injunction, however often it is violated. It is more likely to be effective, of course, if it is reinforced by interest. And positive obligations, like those that I am discussing now, probably require even greater reinforcement. We need to grasp their political dimension, the way they connect with our efforts to achieve security, stability, and peace. There is nothing wrong with insisting that even a morally driven transfer of resources should meet the test of cost-benefit analysis. Indeed, the commitment to weigh consequences is a feature of one of the key Western moral traditions, which may even be, if its various versions are taken together, the dominant tradition: utilitarianism.[11]

Consequentialist argument also stands well within our religious traditions. In Catholic just war theory, for example, the considerations of probability (can the war be won?) and proportionality obviously involve a calculation of costs and benefits. It is rarely possible to provide any precise account of the likelihood of achieving just results or the probable price of those results, but some rough sense of what the figures might be is critically important in political and military decisionmaking. So costs and benefits are deeply embedded in our moral judgments about just and unjust warfare, whether those judgments are made in religious or secular terms. They should also play a central part in our judgments about justice in foreign aid. Who is best equipped to make such judgments? Arguments about probability and risk are most likely to be accurate if they are carried out by men and women who are worldly, skeptical, and iconoclastic and who are able to think outside the constraints of religious doctrine and political ideology. A certain kind of "realism," operating within morality rather than against it, is a necessary feature of political decision-making, and this has been recognized by religious thinkers (like Reinhold Niebuhr) as well as by secularists. When we make war, and when we redistribute resources around the globe, we need to have what might be called, however we come by it, a moral or religious faith in the future of humanity. At the same time, our policies must be guided by an utterly realistic account of humanity's present condition.

Moral Realism and the Iraq War

I would like now to illustrate that moral realism with a critical examination of the U.S. war with Iraq. I will repeat and defend arguments that I made before the war was fought and while it was being fought, but I am able to write now with the benefit of hindsight.

It is probably best to begin with what this war wasn't: it was not a war designed to redistribute resources, either for the benefit of the Iraqi people or for the benefit of American companies. There may be benefits of both these sorts, the first just, the second unjust, but they were not reasons for going to war. The Leninist theory of imperialism argues for reasons of the second sort, but the benefits to the American economy were too uncertain and too limited compared with the costs and risks for the country as a whole: the theory doesn't compute.

Nor was the war an example of humanitarian intervention. Back in 1991, when Saddam Hussein was carrying out a policy of mass murder in the Shi'ite south, a military intervention to stop the killing would probably have been justified. Twelve years later, in 2003, justification was much harder. There were many good reasons for removing Saddam from power, but in the absence of ongoing massacres, the reasons didn't have the urgency that is required to make war a morally necessary recourse. As long as Saddam was in power, of course, the possibility of future massacres loomed on the horizon. But this was a danger that could be dealt with, that arguably was being dealt with, by coercive measures short of war. The no-fly zone in the north was a kind of humanitarian intervention, which effectively protected the lives of Iraq's Kurds (and which produced a kind of regime change: the creation of an autonomous Kurdistan). But this effectiveness was an argument against a full-scale war.

The Bush administration fought the war for the sake of regime change in Iraq and, possibly, in the hopes of a much wider transformation of Arab politics. But the argument in the fall of 2002 and the winter of 2003 was focused on weapons of mass destruction. This was not an accident. Regime change has never commanded much support as a just cause. I will come back to it later on; I have to address first the questions that all the world was debating in the months before the war: What kind of a threat did Iraq pose to regional and global peace? And what degree of imminence or danger might justify a military attack? We know now (as of the winter of 2004) that Iraq did not have usable weapons of mass destruction or even the ingredients necessary to produce them. But political and moral argument is always time-bound; we are responsible for what we knew then or for what we could have known.

It made a lot of sense, before the war, to think that Saddam possessed chemical and biological weapons and was some years away, but not decades away, from possessing nuclear weapons. The UN inspectors had catalogued Iraq's stocks of dangerous materials in the late 1990s, and there was no evidence of the disposal or destruction of those stocks. The brutality of the Baathist regime generally took more primitive forms, but it had used chemical weapons in the past, against Iranians and Kurds. Moreover, Saddam was not only a brutal but also a capricious and reckless dictator, who had launched two wars, at enormous cost to his own people and to neighboring peoples. Iraq in his hands was a "rogue" state.

The threat to regional peace was or seemed to be real, but as with the threat to the Kurds inside Iraq, it could be dealt with, and it was being dealt with, by forceful measures short of war. The coercive constraint of Iraq had three aspects: first, the embargo of military supplies; second, the no-fly zones; and third, the UN inspections. The containment regime was established after the first Gulf War and, except for the inspectors, had been in place ever since; the inspectors withdrew in 1999. Both the embargo and the no-fly zones were chiefly the work of the United States, and the absence of European cooperation turned out to be a significant factor in the lead-up to the war. Had containment been a genuinely inter-nationalist effort, it would have been much harder for the United States to abandon it unilaterally. But such an effort would have required a much wider recognition of the threat that Saddam posed. Instead, much of the world, and especially the French, Germans, and Russians, Iraq's major trading partners, were eager for business-as-usual in the Persian Gulf. This readiness led them very quickly to oppose the war; it also made it impossible for them to stop the war: they were not sufficiently engaged, politically or militarily.

In any case, the truth was that containment was working and should not have been abandoned. I don't mean that deterrence was working—as many critics of the war claimed. Coercive containment did not depend on the threat of force. It required the daily use of force to stop ships on the high seas and to bomb antiaircraft and radar facilities. The UN inspectors were readmitted to Iraq in 2002 because of the threat of force, but that wasn't deterrence; the return of the inspectors was the result of straight-forward coercion. A little war was being fought everyday around and over Iraqi territory, and this was the real alternative to the attack of March 2003. Advocates of a big war argued that the little war could not be sus-tained. But it had already been sustained for a long time, and there were ways to intensify it without accepting the risks of full-scale fighting. It would have been more sustainable, obviously, if containment had been a multilateral project.

The strongest argument against containment was that the new de-structive technologies posed a novel danger: weapons of mass destruction could be deployed very quickly, delivered in minutes, or conveyed in secret to nonstate organizations. The possession or even the possible possession of such weapons, it was said, warranted a preventive war. President George W. Bush talked of preemption, but the argument was actually about pre-vention. Administration officials described an imminent threat, but their real claim was that even if the threat were distant and uncertain, it was suf-ficiently great to warrant immediate action.

We now know that coercive containment had been highly effective, so that the threat was in fact distant, uncertain, and not very great. But even given the knowledge available at the time, the risks of war should have looked greater than the risks involved in sustaining the containment regime. And, again, there were means available to increase the severity and forcefulness of the regime. This should have been the argument of the antiwar movement and also of the French and German governments: that coercive containment, multilaterally enforced, was a better choice than war. "Better choice" would not, indeed, have been an easy argument to march with. What do you write on the placards? What slogans do you shout? But the truth is that most of the antiwar protestors, and most of the governments opposed to the war, were not prepared for coercion of any sort. The international campaign against the war was based on the idea that there was no threat at all. Given the knowledge then available, this was neither a plausible nor a responsible position. And yet, the war was unnecessary. Given that same knowledge, it was right to oppose it.

Unnecessary wars are almost always unjust wars. Still, the most attractive defense of this war was the description of it as a "war of choice," fought for the sake of democracy—in fulfillment, one might say, of the fourth of my posited obligations. The war against Iraq was chosen (out of all the imaginable wars for democracy) because it was possible: here was a vulnerable regime, whose brutality was widely known, whose overthrow would be welcomed by most of its subjects, and whose democratic replacement would be a beacon of light in one of the darker parts of the world. The Anglo-American army would be like the Red Army advancing on Warsaw in 1919—a revolutionary force. This was morality turned militant, and it made for a high-stakes politics. The war was a kind of crusade, a secular and democratic jihad. And then it is understandable that men and women trained, as Bryan Hehir and I are trained, in the antijihadist arguments of just war theory would have no stomach for it. Difference of religion is not a just cause of war, Vitoria argued; nor is difference of politics. There are other ways to pursue political differences, and even in the case of very bad regimes, these ways stop short of war (as long as the badness stops short of mass murder).

But once the war had begun, it made sense even for opponents of the war to hope for a quick defeat of the Baathist regime—and for a democratic replacement, however hard this was to imagine. And for those of us who had argued for multilateralism before the war, it also made sense to hope for a multilateralist occupation of Iraq and for a transitional process shaped by the United Nations. Indeed, the campaign against the war should never have been only an antiwar campaign. It should have been a campaign for a strong international system, designed and organized to defeat aggression, control weapons of mass destruction, stop massacres and ethnic cleansing, and assist in the politics of transition after brutal regimes have been overthrown. But an international system of this sort has to be the work of many different states, not of one state. There have to be many agents ready to take responsibility for the success of the system, not just one.

Multilateralism is a good creed for moral realists: it is just and prudent. After the Iraq war, America's military superiority is indisputable. We possess something close to absolute power, at least in the military sphere. But power of this sort is dangerous, not only for other countries but also for the country that possesses it. Absolute power corrupts: Lord Acton's famous maxim isn't a cliché because it has been repeated so often but rather because it has proved true so often. Overwhelming strength breeds arrogance and imperiousness. This is the moral critique of the position America occupies in the world today. Absolute power also makes people stupid. This is the pragmatic critique. The work of negotiation and persuasion that is necessary in a world where power is more widely shared produces a kind of collective intelligence, which is wisdom in international affairs. And when the work is unnecessary, there is less wisdom. And so powerful states and leaders need other people around to tell them when they are behaving badly or foolishly. The United States today needs partners, not followers, but real partners, who can say yes and no to its policies, with whom it is necessary to argue about questions of morality and politics, negotiate common policies, and work out compromises.

Some of these compromises will, no doubt, be worse than the initial position of one or the other party. Partners can make mistakes together, just as individual actors can make mistakes alone. Still, on balance, over time, arrogance, zeal, and ignorance are more likely to be curbed than furthered by alliances, treaties, and international organizations. A strong multilateralism is worth working for. It is a mistake, however, to pretend that its institutions and practices already exist and are widely effective. That is what France and Germany did in the run-up to the Iraq war, which is why they were incapable of preventing the war. The pretense was and is irresponsible, but the work of partnership is politically and morally crucial.

Notes

1. See the official history: Sir Charles Webster and Noble Frankland, *The Strategic Air Offensive against Germany* (London: Her Majesty's Stationery Office, 1961). C. P. Snow's *Science and Government* (Harvard University Press, 1962) provides a useful, critical, and unofficial version of the story.

2. The essay can be found in Richard Wasserstrom, ed., *War and Morality* (Wadsworth, 1970).

3. See Judah Halevi, *The Kuzari: An Argument for the Faith of Israel*, translated by Hartwig Hirschfeld (Schocken, 1964), p. 111. See Plato, *The Republic*, I: 352.

4. Baruch Spinoza, *Tractatus Theologico-Politicus*, translated by Samuel Shirley (Leiden: E. J. Brill, 1991), p. 94.

5. For a historical account, see James Turner Johnson, *Just War Tradition and the Restraint of War: A Moral and Historical Inquiry* (Princeton University Press, 1981).

6. See my essay "The Triumph of Just War Theory (and the Dangers of Success)," *Social Research* 69 (Winter 2002).

7. Francisco de Vitoria, *Political Writings*, edited by Anthony Pagden and Jeremy Lawrance (Cambridge University Press, 1991), pp. 302–04.

8. For more extensive discussions, see J. L. Holzgrefe and Robert O. Keohane, eds., *Humanitarian Intervention* (Cambridge University Press, 2003). A fuller version of my own position can be found in "Arguing for Humanitarian Intervention," *Dissent* (Winter, 2002); see also Nicolaus Mills and Kira Brunner, eds., *The New Killing Fields: Massacre and the Politics of Intervention* (Basic Books, 2002).

9. Ralph Waldo Emerson, *The Complete Essays and Other Writings*, edited by Brooks Atkinson (Modern Library, 1940), p. 152.

10. For some early salvos, see the essays collected in Thomas W. Pogge, ed., *Global Justice* (Oxford: Blackwell, 2001).

11. Peter Singer makes a strong utilitarian case for global redistribution in *One World: The Ethics of Globalization* (Yale University Press, 2002).

FIGHTING AGAINST TERRORISM
AND FOR JUSTICE

LOUISE RICHARDSON

IF THERE IS an academic equivalent of bringing coals to Newcastle, then commenting on the words of Bryan Hehir and Michael Walzer on faith, morals, and foreign policy must be it. Few people have spoken with such care, erudition, and insight on this subject. I cannot resist the feeling that if only our foreign policy were in their hands, and the hands of people like them, then the world would be a better and an altogether safer place for all of us.

I come to this subject less as a moral thinker and more as someone who thinks about the subject that our administration declared to be the organizing principle of our foreign policy: terrorism and counterterrorism. Organizing our government and our society in the face of the threat posed to us by the architects of the September 11 attacks prompts real questions about how we can fashion a response that is both efficacious and morally defensible.

Faith, Morals, and Foreign Terrorists

Hehir rightly points out that a discussion of "faith, morals, and foreign policy" would not have taken place outside monastic walls or ivory towers thirty years ago. Politics in recent times has been accepted as being an entirely secular affair. Though Michael Walzer convincingly argues that political arguments are often a façade for moral commitments, even within the academy the role of religion in politics has long been largely ignored.[1] As it happens, this secularization of our society is mirrored in the terrorist groups we have encountered. If one were to make a list of the known terrorist groups operating thirty years ago, for example, one would find that none had religious motives, or even a mixture of religious and political motives. The mixture of religious and political motives, long the hallmark of ancient terrorist groups like the Zealots, the Assassins, or the Thugi, was absent from modern terrorist groups until the 1980s when the influence of the Iranian revolution began to take hold.[2] The ideological inspiration of the Iranian revolution, added to the organizational lessons of the war against the Soviet Union in Afghanistan, and the political inspiration derived from the defeat of the Soviet Union and the U.S. withdrawal from Lebanon, all fueled the growth of terrorist movements with a religious agenda.

This is not to suggest that the terrorist groups of the 1970s were benign entities; they were not. If one were to compile a list of known terrorist groups operative in the 1970s, one would notice a large number of social revolutionary groups like the Red Brigades in Italy, the Red Army Faction in Germany, and Action Direct in France, to name only the most notable. These groups too had transformational aspirations. Peopled often by the disaffected children of privilege and motivated by an acute sense of alienation from the rampant injustices in the world, they sought to overthrow capitalism and replace it with an ill-defined but utopian, just, and classless society. The means they adopted to achieve this end was to kill capitalists and their collaborators, in other words, noncombatants.

Whether ideology for social revolutionary movements plays the same role as religion does for fundamentalist groups remains a fascinating and largely unexplored question. Both revolutionary ideology and fundamentalist religion have required complete commitment of the individual, provided answers to all questions, promised a better future, and required transformation of the existing order. Just as Walzer argues that his four propositions for a moral foreign policy can be derived from both religious and secular traditions, and fulfilled under the auspices of either, so the revolutionary agenda of transformational terrorists can probably be derived from and consistent with both religious and atheist ideologies. However, the more traditional, numerous, long-lasting, and geographically dispersed, ethnonationalist terrorist groups have been of an entirely different ilk. They have had concrete political aspirations, which are often widely shared and in many instances negotiable.

The appearance of terrorist groups with religious motivations actually harkens back to an older pre–French Revolutionary world when all terrorist groups possessed a mixture of religious and political motives. Religious groups, however, shared two characteristics that have set them apart from other terrorist groups. First, they have exercised less restraint. Terrorists generally have not taken the opportunities open to them to kill large numbers of people. They have not needed to inflict mass casualties to communicate their political message by terrorizing a population. Familiar with the old Chinese adage "kill 1, frighten 10,000," they have generally killed small numbers. The Irish Republican Army (IRA), for example, could plant a bomb outside Harrods Department store in December 1983, thereby killing five people and terrorizing most of the inhabitants of London. It did not need to plant the bomb in the middle of the summer sale in Harrods Food Court and thereby kill hundreds of people. Had the IRA done so it would have alienated its audience at home on whom it relied for political and logistical support. If the audience is God, however, there is no need to exercise restraint, and religious terrorists generally have not done so. Instead, they have carefully tried to kill the largest number of people possible, as the September 11 attacks, and the earlier attack on the World Trade Center in 1993, were clearly designed to do. In this way their violence is reminiscent of the expressive anticolonialist rage described by Frantz Fanon and quite unlike the carefully calibrated violence of most other terrorist groups.[3]

Religious terrorist movements have also been transnational. In this sense al Qaeda curiously belongs in the same category as IBM, the World Bank, and the Jesuits. Religious demarcations have often not corresponded to political boundaries, and religious terrorist groups have operated across borders, drawing supporters and sponsors from different countries. This has enabled them to last longer than others and to be more difficult to defeat. Al Qaeda, with its loose networks of affiliated organizations and the connections fostered through the diaspora of militants from the jihadist training camps of Afghanistan, is a prime example of such capability. Finally, religious terrorist groups are not now, and never have been, the sole preserve of Islam, as evidenced by the work of Jewish extremists in Israel or the Aum Shinriko cult in Japan.

Just as there are differences between types of terrorist groups, there are very real differences in the role religion plays for different groups. Broadly, I believe religion serves one of three different functions in terrorist groups. For many groups religion is simply the badge of ethnic identity. Religion helps one to define oneself and identify one's enemy, but groups are not fighting about doctrinal differences. This is clearly the case in the Northern Irish conflict. Religion has made the problem more intractable and has rendered efforts to integrate the two communities more difficult, but religious doctrine has no importance in the problem. The leaderships of both major churches involved have long tried to resolve the conflict.

The second, and by far the most common, role religion plays in terrorist groups is as a tool for recruitment, a mask for political motives, and a means of acquiring or claiming legitimacy. This is the corollary of the argument Walzer makes that strategic arguments in politics are driven by unacknowledged moral convictions. Take the example of Hamas. The charter of Hamas and the literature of the organization is suffused with religious rhetoric. Yet the actions of Hamas do not reflect any religious imperative but rather are driven by the very political desire of Hamas to displace the Palestine Liberation Organization (PLO) as the legitimate voice of the Palestinians. In these cases religion is wittingly or unwittingly used as a tool of politics, just as the realists say of the relationship between states and religion.

Religion can also be used as an alternative claim to legitimacy and sovereignty, an ideology or theory, or a guide to action. This is most often true in religious cults such as the Aum Shinriko group, which released sarin gas in the Tokyo subway in March 1995. Like the ancient Indian Thugi, Shoko Asahara, the leader of Aum Shinriko, was a devotee of the goddess Kali. Her followers believe that the goddess is pleased by the brutal murder of travelers, preferably without shedding their blood. The Thugi interpreted this to warrant the murder, by strangling with a silk scarf, of non-European travelers. Asahara believed it to warrant the murder, by chemical or biological weapons (he experimented with both), of travelers on the Tokyo subway.

I have to confess that it is a little unclear into which of these categories al Qaeda fits. We do not understand the movement well enough to know the relative weights of the religious and political motivations of the group. My hunch is that they belong in the second category, and to support this hunch I point to the evolution of the various publications issued by al Qaeda. The invocation of the ignominy of Israel, for example, which barely merited a mention in early statements, gradually appeared more and more often as Israeli unpopularity was clearly seen as a means of mobilizing support for the cause. The extent of our ignorance of al Qaeda, of its operations, motives, appeal, and recruitment strategy is certainly a damning indictment of people like me who study these groups and, more to the point, of our intelligence services who have a lot more resources than scholars to investigate these groups. So we genuinely do not know what the relative weight for al Qaeda is of the millenarianist claims that they make in comparison with the very pragmatic political claims that they also make.

The question for us becomes, what are we to do in the face of an enemy whose actions violate every norm of what we consider civilized behavior, and who, unlike previous terrorists, are clearly trying to kill as many innocent noncombatants as possible? This is an enormously difficult question. It is rendered more difficult by the absence of a body of international law that can guide us through our campaign against terrorists.

The first thing I believe we have to do is to understand our opponent. There is a tendency to see all religious terrorist groups as an undifferentiated mass of religious fanatics. In fact there are very real differences among terrorist groups and even among religious terrorist groups. I am convinced that if we are ever to fashion an effective policy against terrorists we must first understand who they are, how they operate, and why they have appeal. Hehir's essay eloquently draws out some of the different strands of thinking in Catholic and Protestant ideologies in this country on the role of morals and foreign policy. We are perfectly prepared to accept these nuances in our own faiths but tend to assume a uniformity of view among those we know less well. As on other issues, simplicity of interpretation tends to increase with distance from the case.

In our depiction of terrorists as simply evil incarnate we mirror the Manichaeism of our opponents. When our president paraphrased Jesus, as quoted in Matthew 12:30, "Those who are not with us are against us," he adopted a starkly bifurcated view, depriving the world of nuance or complexity.[4] Even a very friendly European diplomat, Javier Solana, the European Union's high representative on foreign affairs, took exception: "It is a kind of binary model. It is all or nothing. For us Europeans, it is difficult to deal with because we are secular. We do not see the world in such black and white terms."[5] Depicting enemies as evil incarnate may help mobilize the domestic population against them, though the atrocity of September 11 was more than enough to do so anyway. It does not help us to understand them or even, ultimately, to defeat them.

The notion that terrorists have no morals or are blinded to moral considerations by their fanatical beliefs is, of course, quite untrue. Nobody makes this point better than Albert Camus in *The Just Assassins*.[6] In this play he tells the story of how Kaliayev, with the support of his coconspirators, refused to kill his target, the Grand Duke Sergei, as to do so would have required him to kill the children traveling with the duke too. Kaliayev, who was executed for terrorism in 1905, explained that he had planned to kill himself along with his victim, Minister Plehva. The members of this Russian anarchist group believed that terrorism was justified when the perpetrator was prepared to sacrifice his own life to atone for the lives he was taking. This is a concept of martyrdom, or "shaheed," not unlike that held by the medieval Assassins, by insurgents in Malabar, Atjeh, and Mindanao in the eighteenth and nineteenth centuries, and by Palestinians, Kurds, and Tamils today. Conversations with terrorists today confirm the view that they believe themselves to be acting morally and believe that history will so judge them. In support they constantly invoke the names of erstwhile terrorists who subsequently became statesmen, Menachem Begin and Nelson Mandela being their most popular examples.

Bin Laden has made repeated public attempts to justify his actions. The act of issuing fatwas is an effort to claim a degree of religious legitimacy for his actions. In his first fatwa, in 1996, bin Laden declared that American troops were legitimate targets because of their occupation of the Islamic holy places. Two years later he issued another fatwa in which he broadened his category of legitimate targets to include American civilians. Again he tried to provide justification for this expansion. First, he argued that since the U.S. public witnessed the actions of the U.S. government yet did not have the will to destroy that government, then the public was, in fact, culpable of the action of the government. His second argument was the argument of moral equivalence. He argued that what he called the U.S. murder of a million Iraqi children by sanctions, and the U.S. bombing of Iraq, which resulted in civilian casualties, meant that the United States murdered civilians too.[7] On other occasions he has pointed to the U.S. bombing of Hiroshima and Nagasaki to legitimize his action against the United States.

Ramzi bin al-Shibh, a senior member of al Qaeda, attempted a detailed justification of the September 11 attacks. He argued that they were legitimate according to *sharia*, because they were committed against a country at war with Muslims and because Muslims are free to attack women, children, and the elderly when their own women, children, and elderly are attacked. He argued further that the benefits, including material losses of "one trillion dollars" and "two thousand economic brains," justified the harm. Finally, in the most chilling part of the document he advised that in killing Americans, "Muslims should not exceed four million noncombatants, or render more than ten million of them homeless. We should avoid this, to make sure the penalty is no more than reciprocal."[8]

Here is the ultimate vicious cycle: bin Laden and his followers argue that America's killing of other civilians justifies their killing of American civilians. Many Americans then appear to believe that justifies U.S. abandonment of the normal moral constraints restraining action against terrorists and terrorist suspects. If you believe, as I do, that these claims to moral equivalence are spurious, and if you believe, as I do, that the United States does, in fact, occupy the moral high ground, then the onus, it seems to me, is on the United States to break this vicious cycle.

Seeing the world and depicting the enemy in black and white terms is a common practice in wartime. Americans have tended to do so too when the war has been cold and the enemy much less than a state. Throughout the cold war America perceived the world as divided between evil communists and moral democrats. In this way we completely blinded ourselves to the complexities of the world in which we lived. We repeatedly saw communism when we should have seen nationalism, and we allied ourselves with brutal regimes, who daily transgressed the norms in which we believe, because they were anticommunist. In so doing we persuaded a great many people, especially those trying to change these authoritarian dictatorships, that we did not believe in the principles we preached. It would be a terrible tragedy inimical to our long-term interests if we were to make the same mistake again.

The last time the threat of terrorism reached the top of the national agenda was the 1980s. The Reagan administration then saw the issue through the prism of anticommunism. The government repeatedly argued that terrorists were the puppets of the states who sponsored them and that the Soviet Union bankrolled terrorism the world over as a means of inflicting harm on the West. Claire Sterling's book was thought to provide the backing for this thinking, and Secretary of State Alexander Haig apparently distributed copies to everyone who entered his office.[9] Although the Soviet Union undoubtedly helped to support a number of left-wing terrorist groups in this period, there was very little empirical basis for the notion of a communist-backed global network of terrorists, but the lack of evidence in no way undermined the tenacity with which the view was held.

We seem to be repeating the pattern. We have replaced communism with Islamic fundamentalism as our bogeyman. In so doing we completely fail to perceive the very real differences between these groups and between these terrorists and others. I believe our ability to understand and exploit these differences is one of the keys to the success of our counterterrorist campaign. If we repeat the cold war pattern of allying ourselves with any government, irrespective of their politics and practices, simply because they share our antipathy to our enemy *du jour*, communism then, terrorism now, we run the risk of jeopardizing our chances of success. Our success depends on our ability to persuade the potential recruits of the terrorists that we hold the moral high ground, that we believe in the principles we espouse, and that the terrorists' view of America is wrong. If our actions seem to be consistent with the arguments of our enemies—that we care only for our own economic well-being, our own rights, and the rights of those subject to our opponents—then we may well lose the argument. In the long term we will lose our ability to win this campaign.

Walzer's Propositions on Intervention

Walzer spells out four propositions about intervention that he convincingly argues are consistent with a just war theory of any hue. I would like to test their pertinence to counterterrorism policy. His first proposition is that in a system of sovereign states, multilateral action is preferable to the action of single states. This is surely also true of counterterrorist actions. Multilateral action has the advantage of being more consistent with the argument that terrorism, and in particular the attacks of September 11, are an attack on humanity rather than an attack just on Americans. In the case of policy against a transnational movement like al Qaeda and its off-spring, moreover, multilateral action is more likely to be effective. Only through agreement to share intelligence, hand over suspects, and often work together on the ground, can these groups be uprooted.

The second proposition, that inconsistency should not preclude action, is also, of course, true when applied to counterterrorist actions. Application of the second proposition could, however, undermine the application of the first, if it transpires that one is only prepared to act against one's own enemies and not the enemies of others.

The third proposition, the doctrine of double effect, that is, unintended consequences of an act, is very difficult to apply to a counterterrorist campaign. The issue is that terrorist acts rarely kill large numbers of people. The terrorist attack of September 11 is unprecedented in human history in its magnitude of destruction of life and property. Terrorists are invariably outmanned and outgunned by their opponents, so their whole strategy is to inflict far greater psychological damage than physical damage. Most military actions against terrorists, therefore, are likely to kill more civilians than were hurt in the original attack. How then does one weigh the psychological damage inflicted on large numbers by the terrorists against the actual loss of life of civilians in the countermeasures? To take an example from April 1986, did the terror inflicted on the patrons of the Berlin discothèque and their families on April 5 justify the deaths of those who lived in the residential district of Tripoli hit accidentally by a U.S. cruise missile fired in retaliation ten days later? I think not.

The counterargument, of course, is that the military action against the terrorists saves future lives of those they might kill. But this is a very difficult equation. In the Libyan case it is unpersuasive because the 1986 bombing of Tripoli did not stop Libyan support of terrorism but rather drove that support underground. Moreover, the bombing of Tripoli resulted in far larger loss of civilian life when the Libyans seeking revenge blew up Pan Am 103 over Lockerbie, Scotland, killing 270 people on December 21, 1988.

Walzer's third proposition imposes very real constraints on the use of the military in a counterterrorist campaign. My sense is that our government and public will not accept those constraints; though I believe that if the United States did so, a counterterrorism campaign over the long term would be altogether more effective.

The fourth proposition, that force as a last resort is not a plausible guide to foreign policy decisionmaking, seems very different when it is applied to a decision to deploy force to stop an ongoing massacre or genocide, than when applied to the deployment of troops against a group of terrorists before they commit another atrocity. In the first case immediate use of force is morally required even if there is some hope that diplomatic action may yield results. In the second case, the action is likely to resemble the kind of extralegal and extraterritorial aggression it is designed to preempt.

Foreign Aid

In his essay Walzer considers foreign aid and the extent of the obligations of the rich to share their wealth with the poor. He recalls the Marshall Plan that he argues, I believe rightly, was driven not by liberal guilt but by enlightened self-interest. He suggests that we use the same arguments of interest in thinking about the rest of the world today.

The difficulty of course is that while an argument on the basis of interest, if convincing, is more likely to be persuasive to policymakers, an argument on the basis of humanitarianism is more convincing. Our friends in the Muslim world constantly invoke the example of the Marshall Plan, when the United States expended 3 percent of its gross domestic product in a financial bailout of western Europe. They have a very hard time, however, explaining how our doing so now would undermine the rampant resentment of our wealth in the region.

There are a number of explanations for the generosity of the United States in 1945 that do not pertain today. I think Walzer is right in arguing that U.S. generosity was indeed driven by enlightened self-interest. At the time, the United States wanted to build up Europe in the belief that only a strong ally was a good ally, and that the United States needed a good ally, preferably one geographically poised as a buffer, in the anticipated conflict with the Soviet Union. American policymakers also believed that the continued growth of the U.S. economy required strong overseas markets and a liberal international economic system, both of which the Marshall Plan was designed to create. Finally, many claims were made to cultural affinities, shared experiences, and traditions to ease the passage of the plan.

Very few of these arguments apply today. Even the strongest proponents of a new Marshall Plan make no claims to cultural affinities, of which, let's face it, there are not many. Arguments based on human affinity are stronger. The arguments on the basis of moral obligation are entirely convincing when they are preached to the choir, but they fall on deaf ears when they are proposed to the policymakers. The argument on the basis of enlightened self-interest remains. The problem with this argument is that it is a tough sell; there is not a lot of readily available empirical evidence in support of it.

There is no doubt that terrorist groups and other violent forces thrive in failed states and that our security would be enhanced if all states had functioning governments in control of the use of violence in their societies. As we are discovering in Afghanistan and Iraq, however, the cost of state building, of creating functioning, credible, and unifying institutions, is enormous. It requires a massive commitment of resources, human and economic, as well as time, patience, and energy. Even then, the odds of success are not great. The odds of persuading the American public of the need to sustain the commitment and the costs are even lower.

An argument based on enlightened self-interest that might stand a chance, if it could be proven, is that alleviating global poverty would eliminate the threat of terrorism. But the link between terrorism and poverty has not been demonstrated, in spite of a great many efforts to do so. The link is definite, but it is a complex one. If there were a direct link between poverty and terrorism, one would expect Africa to be awash in terrorism, but it is not. The fact is that the number of terrorists the world over is tiny, so it is difficult to explain the actions of small numbers of individuals or groups with broad-based explanations. A great many people experience the same objective conditions, and only a very few become terrorists. That said, there can be little doubt that the impoverished refugee camps of the Middle East have served as spawning grounds for recruits to terrorist movements.

Social revolutionary terrorism we know to have emerged primarily in the wealthy industrialized societies of the West. Ethnonationalist terrorism, rather than manifesting itself in the poorest societies, has often emerged in regions or among ethnic groups that are relatively well off. This is as true of the Tamils in Sri Lanka as the Sikhs in India and the Basques in Spain. The concept of relative deprivation associated with Ted Robert Gurr has been most helpful.[10] His theory is that when economic conditions improve, expectations tend to rise faster, and that people tend to rebel when there is a gap between their expectations, based on their relative condition, and their capacity to satisfy them.

Terrorists do indeed thrive in failed states. They also thrive when they have powerful and generous state sponsors. They also manage to survive and inflict harm without the benefits of either. Terrorism is above all a tactic, and it has proved a relatively effective one in the hands of the weak against the strong precisely because it is so versatile and can be employed by small numbers of people lacking significant resources.

Walzer argues, and I fear that he is right in saying, that we will not solve the critical problems of famine, disease, exploitation, and persecution as long as we continue to see them only in humanitarian terms. I am not too sanguine, however, about the possibility of convincing our leaders or their followers that it is in their interest to do so. The argument would require convincing the publics of the West that high costs should be borne now in the hope of reaping benefits to our security later. Unfortunately the experience of our democracy, as witnessed by the current attitude to budget deficits, is to reap the benefits now and pass the costs along to bear later.

Iraq

Walzer applies what he calls "moral realism" to the war in Iraq. He maintains that there were alternatives to the war and concludes that there was no just cause for fighting it. He also rejects the blinded simplicity of much of the antiwar movement who chose to ignore the realities of Hussein's brutal regime. Instead he characteristically makes an altogether more nuanced case for coercive diplomacy against Iraq. His argument which, like most of his arguments, I find entirely convincing, is nevertheless an extremely difficult one to make, especially in a media age that prefers simplicity to nuance. Walzer argues for enforcing the embargo, the no-fly zone, and the inspections system as an alternative to war. He rightly concedes the difficulty of mobilizing behind this policy. "What do you write on the placards?" he asks. He argues for a campaign for a strong international system designed to guarantee the physical security of all the world's people. This is indeed a placard well worth marching behind. That it would undoubtedly be dismissed as utopian should not in itself prevent the march.

The alleged link between Saddam Hussein and al Qaeda was one of the most powerful arguments in favor of war. It was the only argument consistent with making war when the United States did. The other argument, Hussein's brutality, was of long standing and had not served as an adequate casus belli in a great many other instances of comparable brutality. The third argument, that he was developing weapons of mass destruction, which we all believed, it now turns out mistakenly, was something that the inspections were designed to prevent. What of this link with terrorism?

Iraq has long occupied a place on the State Department's list of state sponsors of terrorism. The country's historical support of certain terrorist groups is well known. But this list is a curious one indeed. It contains countries like Cuba, who in recent years have done little more than provide safe haven to some superannuated leftist leaders, and countries like Iran, which has in the past and continues today to guide and bankroll some of the most active, brutal, and dangerous terrorist groups in the world. Meanwhile the one country, outside of Afghanistan, with the closest links to al Qaeda, Saudi Arabia, did not appear on the list at all. Even Afghanistan did not appear on the list. The only possible justification for this omission, though not one used by the State Department, is that rather than being a state sponsor of a terrorist group, Afghanistan was a state sponsored by a terrorist group. Walzer's point, that an inconsistent application of policy is better than no application, is well taken; but in this instance, the compilation of this list, which has real world significance in the way of mandated sanctions for those on it, has no legitimacy. The list is compiled with as close an eye to domestic American politics as to the links between states and sponsors. There is therefore no reason anyone should accept it as legitimate. If the United States is to produce a list of state sponsors of terrorism, it should articulate criteria for inclusion and apply them consistently.

The Bush administration repeatedly argued that the link between al Qaeda and Saddam Hussein was beyond doubt and was one of the prime motives for war. Secretary of State Colin Powell spelled out this argument in greatest detail in his speech to the United Nations.[11] The fact is, of course, that this link has never been proven and, given what we know of al Qaeda, is highly unlikely. Although Americans have tended to see themselves as the prime target of radical Islamic groups, in fact, the more immediate targets have long been the secular governments in the region. Their enmity toward America initially derived from the fact that U.S. support has kept many of these regimes in place. These regimes do not share America's commitment to democracy and routinely violate the human and civil rights of their citizens.

While the United States was undoubtedly on bin Laden's long list of enemies, so was Saddam Hussein. When Hussein invaded Kuwait in 1993, bin Laden approached the Saudi royal family and offered to mobilize the mujahadeen who had fought so successfully in Afghanistan to expel Hussein from Iraq. The Saudis declined and instead did the unforgivable, in bin Laden's eyes, by inviting the infidel Americans into the region to expel Saddam Hussein. Far from Hussein and bin Laden being allies, therefore, they were sworn enemies. Had we taken the elementary step of trying to understand our opponents we would have appreciated this irony. Not for the first time, we may well be in the throes of creating a self-fulfilling prophecy. Bin Laden's recent pronouncements have called for support of the Iraqis against the Americans, and his followers are undoubtedly exploiting the lawlessness of Iraq to enter the country and take potshots at American troops. Just as enmity toward the Soviet Union drew the United States into the curious alliance with the mujahadeen,

U.S. enmity toward bin Laden and Hussein is now, in all likelihood, drawing their followers together.

A Just Campaign against Terrorism

I am of the opinion that in this instance, in this campaign against terrorists, if not necessarily in all others, the most efficacious response is also the most ethical.[12] I believe that the campaign against terrorists is not one that can be won by military means. The history of antiterrorist campaigns is fairly unequivocal on this point. It is fundamentally a political and psychological conflict, and it has to be fought, and can only be won, on those terms. The worldview of Osama bin Laden and his followers is so diametrically opposed to that of America and so transformational in its intent that I see little or no point in trying to negotiate with him. The focus of America's attention ought to be on the potential recruits of these terrorist organizations and on those whose silent complicity is enough to permit these organizations to thrive. Our goal should be to win their support. The experience of other counterterrorist campaigns suggests that once the groups are isolated, they are a great deal easier to defeat by means of the traditional and legitimate application of state power.

We can achieve this goal by demonstrating in our response to the ghastly atrocity visited upon us that we mean what we say when we say that we believe in the rule of law and the value of democratic principles. We can do this in a variety of ways. We do it by holding our friends to the same standards as we hold our enemies. We can do this by limiting our punishment to the evildoers, refusing to participate in the cycle of violence into which the terrorists are trying to provoke us, and refusing to fall victim to the most common motive of the terrorist—the desire for revenge. We can do this by using our wealth constructively to drain the swamps in which these groups grow, the impoverished Palestinian refugee camps and the jihadist-training madrassahs in Pakistan. We can do this by demonstrating our commitment to the rule of law domestically and internationally by acting through international institutions, using international tribunals to try our opponents, and permitting ourselves to be constrained in our treatment of our captives by international conventions on the rules of warfare and treatment of prisoners. We should use this situation as an opportunity to reaffirm our belief in international law. We could also have a firm declaratory policy that nobody has a right deliberately to kill innocent civilians to achieve political aims and that we will oppose whoever does so. If we declare this policy, and hold ourselves and our friends to it, we have some hope of winning the argument with the potential recruits of the terrorists.

It is probably not enough to act ethically to win this argument. We must engage in the argument. It is not enough that we attempt to avoid civilian casualties; we must make every effort to ensure that the world knows we are doing so. We should be waging a campaign of public diplomacy with the same skill, relentlessness, and resources as we are prepared to commit to a military campaign in the Islamic world.

In the period since September 11 we have witnessed very little public debate on an ethical response to terrorism. We have been concerned, I fear, primarily with what works, not what is right. We have witnessed an almost Orwellian misuse of the English language, most grotesquely in the USA Patriot Act. The distinctions we have drawn among enemies, from citizens, to resident aliens, to foreigners, seem to me not to have been based on efforts to draw moral distinctions but rather to come up with names to justify whatever treatments we care to administer. The public is clearly frightened, so we cannot rely on an aroused public to hold our leadership accountable. There was virtually no outcry in November 2002, for example, when an unmanned American Predator drone blew up a car in Yemen carrying an al Qaeda suspect and five other people whom our government could not identify at the time. Apparently this killing did not violate our prohibition against assassination because we simply refrained from calling it assassination.

In thinking about what underlying principles should guide our choice of action it seems to me that the tradition of U.S. involvement overseas is not a bad place to start. One principle is that we should not claim a right to ourselves that we are not prepared to concede to others. This would be an argument against the policy of preemption contained in the new national security doctrine. On this I agree entirely with Hehir. During the Cuban missile crisis, when there was a call for a preemptive strike against

Cuba at a time this country was facing a far stronger enemy than we face today, Robert Kennedy responded, "For 175 years we have not been that kind of country." I think that too is a good guiding principle, though an entirely secular one, to keep in mind.[13] These principles that ought to guide us, the principles of restraint, noncombatant immunity, and belief in the rule of law, are all derivable from many religious traditions. Our task should be to mobilize people of all religions traditions behind them.

The attack on the World Trade Center was an extraordinary atrocity in the heart of America's most populous city. But it was more than an attack on Americans. In choosing their target, the terrorists chose not just a symbol of the United States but a symbol of the Western economic system. It was indeed, as our leaders said at the time, a crime against humanity, not least because of the 500 victims from 80 countries who died, in addition to the 2,300 Americans. The nature of the attack, however, also provided us with an extraordinary opportunity to mobilize the international community against the use of terrorism and in favor of a stronger international system. In the period immediately after the attack, countries throughout the world offered help and assistance. As Hehir points out, the attack was adjudged to legitimize an American invocation of article 51 of the United Nations Charter. More than 160 countries froze the assets of terrorists and their supporters. Twenty countries provided direct military support to the U.S. operation in Afghanistan. In the period since then we have squandered this remarkable opportunity to mobilize behind the kind of placard Walzer describes. By ignoring the reservations of the international community, refusing to heed the advice of our friends in the region who argued against the invasion of Iraq, and refusing to be bound by the internationally accepted prohibitions on intervention, we have acted in a manner far easier to square with the terrorists' explanation of our motives than with our own. We have, moreover, created a self-fulfilling prophecy by mobilizing waves of new recruits for the terrorist movements of the region. The tragedy of September 11 has been compounded by our failure to adhere to a set of firmly held and widely shared principles on the proper conduct of our foreign policy, our refusal to allow ourselves to be constrained by the international community, and our failure to seize the opportunity afforded by this atrocity to build a stronger international system.

Notes

1. In *Revolutions in Sovereignty: How Ideas Shaped Modern International Relations* (Princeton University Press, 2001), Daniel Philpott surveys the journals *International Organization, International Security, International Studies Quarterly,* and *World Politics* and finds only a handful of articles, out of many hundreds published, featuring religion.

2. For the seminal work on these groups see David Rapoport, "Fear and Trembling: Terrorism in Three Religious Traditions," *American Political Science Review,* vol. 78 (July 1984), pp. 658–77.

3. Frantz Fanon, *The Wretched of the Earth* (Grove Press, 1963).

4. The president made this statement repeatedly as, for example, at a press conference with President Jacques Chirac on November 6, 2001.

5. Quoted in the *Financial Times,* January 8, 2003, p. 14.

6. Albert Camus, *Les Justes* (Gallimard, 1950).

7. For a collection of bin Laden statements in translation see Barry Rubin and Judith Colp Rubin, eds., *Anti-American Terrorism and the Middle East: A Documentary Reader* (Oxford University Press, 2002).

8. See excerpts of a document entitled "The Truth About the New Crusade" in Alan Cullison, "Inside Al-Qaeda's Hard Drive," *Atlantic Monthly,* vol. 294, no. 2 (September 2004), pp. 55–70.

9. Claire Sterling, *The Terrorist Network* (Rhinehart and Winston, 1981).

10. Ted Robert Gurr, *Why Men Rebel* (Princeton University Press, 1971). See also Gurr's more recent *Peoples versus States: Minorities at Risk in the New Century* (U.S. Institute of Peace, 2000).

11. Secretary Colin L. Powell, "Remarks to the United Nations Security Council," New York City, February 5, 2003.

12. Note that I prefer to speak of a campaign against terrorists than of a war on terrorism. There are a great many reasons why I believe war to be a mistaken metaphor in this instance, but that is an argument for another day.

13. As quoted by his brother, Senator Edward M. Kennedy, at his induction into the American Academy of Arts and Letters, October 5, 2002, Cambridge, Mass. See also Ernest R. May and Philip D. Zelikow, eds., *The Kennedy Tapes: Inside the White House during the Cuban Missile Crisis* (Harvard University Press, 1997), pp. 189, 207.

BETWEEN FAITH AND ETHICS

SHIBLEY TELHAMI

IN THIS CHAPTER, I address four related issues: the role of religion in world politics and in American foreign policy, the sources of political power of religious groups and organizations, the relations between religious and ethical beliefs and foreign policy, and the relationship between the ethical and the religious. I end by drawing specific conclusions about American foreign policy.

Faith or Organization?

In the discourse about religion and politics, there is often a lack of differentiation between the role of religious ideas and the role of religious organizations. Although ideas often have an impact on political debates and policies, it is clear, as Charles Krauthammer correctly points out in this volume, that religious leaders may learn contradictory lessons from the same religious text. It is more generally true that the proposition that religion plays an increasingly important role in politics in certain parts of the world refers especially to the greater prominence of religious organizations in society and politics.

Clearly, when political systems have not allowed the proliferation of political opposition, religious organizations, with their capacity to organize and mobilize the masses, have often moved to fill the political vacuum. The rising power of Islamic political movements in Arab and Muslim countries in recent decades, for example, has been very much a function of the superior organizational capabilities of religious groups and the absence of legitimate alternative organizations that challenge authoritarian regimes.

Similarly, in Latin America, the Philippines, and Poland, the Roman Catholic Church's power to mobilize opposition to authoritarian governments can be explained more fully by its organizational capacity in a closed political environment than by the content of faith of its religious communities. Even in more democratic states, where nonreligious organizational capacities exist, the strength of religious organizations is central in explaining the degree of political power each group wields. It is not a surprise that early African American political leadership emerged out of the African American churches that have had the best ability to mobilize communities that have had limited access to mainstream American political organizations. The power of African American churches remains, but as African Americans have acquired more access to the political mainstream, the power of churches has somewhat diminished.

Another example from America is telling. If one contrasts the relative role of Jewish and Arab organizations in American politics, one sees that religious organizations are central in mobilizing people at the community level. To be sure many differences exist between the two groups that explain the relative success of Jewish groups and the relative weakness of Arab groups, including generational differences, socioeconomic levels, and issues that mobilize each community. But even aside from the level of political organization that each side has, religious organizations loom large in people's lives. Although most American Jews are secular, most of them have some cultural or religious affiliation with a synagogue. The synagogue becomes for them a focal point of information about issues that bear on a collective identity, including political issues and especially ones related to Israel. It means that politicians, local and national, have a ready-made platform from which to appeal to a broad constituency. Inevitably, the religious and the political come together.

In contrast, most Arab Americans are Christian. Although some have relations with local Christian Arab churches, most inevitably belong to other, non-Arab churches. Thus their sense of community, and their organizational capacity as Arabs, is very different from the experience of American Jews. Most Muslim Americans are not Arab. It is estimated that fewer than 10 percent of them are affiliated with mosques. In short, the level of religious organization has a direct bearing on the effectiveness of a community's political organization. All of this, of course, is entirely separate from the issue of faith.

As a final note related to American politics, clearly when one speaks of the role of religion in America today, one is especially speaking of the role of some of the evangelical churches that have become powerful within the Republican Party. But although their appeal to their members is framed in theological terms, the actual power of these churches in America is obviously strictly organizational. About a quarter of Americans identify themselves as "born again" Christians.[1] Many of them do not agree with the sort of vision proposed by influential evangelical ministers such as Jerry Falwell and Pat Robertson. The political alliance that has emerged between these groups and some conservative Jewish groups, despite the many important differences between them, makes it clear that their source of power is less often the power of religious ideas and more often the power of religious and political organizations. Historically, the rise and expansion of evangelical movements in America have also depended on their appeal to disenfranchised segments of society, to whom they have reached out through various mediums, including the traditional traveling churches and, more recently, television.

From this perspective, religious groups, whatever their beliefs, have the right to organize themselves and attempt to influence policy at home and abroad, as long as they do not violate the basic rules about separation of church and state in America. We must treat the place of religious organizations in American politics in the same way we treat that of any other organization: as long as they abide by the law, they are part of the political landscape. Those traditional religious organizations that are unhappy about the privileged role that some evangelical organizations play in the name of Christianity must find a way to compete if they want their views reflected in the policy discourse.

Although in my judgment the focus on organizations should be a starting point, questions remain that in some way drive the current debate about the power of religion in America. Importantly, what is the role of faith in the strength of religious organizations? And does the appeal to religion by these groups translate into the moral high ground?

SHIBLEY TELHAMI

The Role of Faith

To argue that the increasing role of religion in politics is more truly a function of organization and political space than of faith is not to say that faith is not a factor. To begin with, the strength of the religious organizations in society partly depends on the strength of faith. Religiosity must always be separated conceptually from the issue of the political clout of religious organizations. In American history, cycles of rising and declining membership in religious groups have occurred, but these fluctuations have not always been related to political clout, at least not directly.

People may join religious organizations for many reasons, but faith is often a factor in their motivation. And clearly passion about one's religious beliefs is sometimes a driving force especially suited to active politics. Whether or not religious leaders who actively pursue political influence are simply aspiring politicians, or truly moved by their faith, clearly their followers are often moved by faith; the most passionately faithful, the most effectively mobilized. This passion often explains why many groups in American politics broadly are often defined by extremist members: effectiveness in American politics is largely about passion. The opinions of most Americans on issues that they do not rank high in their priorities matter little for their own behavior and thus for the behavior of American politicians. Those who care most deeply about an issue to vote on its basis, contribute to political campaigns, and rally are those who matter most to the shaping of political views on that issue. Passion is power in American politics.

Passionate belief, whether secular or religious, simultaneously explains the potential role that religious groups can play and the reason why religious and secular political groups in America are often defined not by the opinions of the majorities among them but by the opinions of the most passionate minorities. This often means more extreme positions exist on issues than a simple public opinion poll may reflect. It is hard to be passionately moderate and thus effective as a moderate in American politics.

Passionate faith is powerful. Is it the driving force of political activism or merely an instrument in the hands of aspiring politicians? At one level, it is obviously impossible to say. At another level, it is easy to see the superiority of political motivation over an assent to faith. A subject of considerable recent interest outside America, political Islam, illustrates the question. In the early 1990s, the second largest Arab town in Israel, Um al-Fahm, which has always had a large devout Muslim community, had a communist mayor, also at a time the communist party in Israel championed Arab rights. The failure of the mayor of Um al-Fahm to deliver the goods locally or nationally was contrasted with the ability of a competing religious leader whose organization provided desperately needed local services, from paving streets to helping build houses. In the following election, the population of Um al-Fahm dumped the communist mayor and elected his deeply religious opponent. It is hard to believe that in a span of four years a quick conversion from atheism to Islam had transpired. Religiosity was obviously not driving the votes, especially since many religious faithful had voted for the communist mayor in the first election. Faith simply could not explain the political rise of religious leadership.

Similarly, in the Islamic revolution in Iran, Islam was strong in Iranian society. That power had been there all along. Islam's political success in 1978 was mostly because other means to organize effective opposition to an unpopular government were largely absent. That does not mean that the faithful can easily separate in their own minds the issue of faith from the issue of political power. Most people instinctively do what works without much serious reflection on the source of success. But some deliberately join a religious group or build a coalition with it as an instrument to fulfill their aims: the secularist Mujahideen Khalq, which had actively opposed the government of the shah, jumped on the bandwagon of the Islamic revolution owing to a simple fact: it did not have a great deal of popular organizational capacity, and the Islamic groups did. Not only did its efforts succeed, but the Iranian public elected the secular head of the party as the first president of the Islamic Republic of Iran, only to see him forced out once the inevitable struggle began between the clergy, headed by the Ayatollah Khomeini, and the secularists. The lesson was clear: the instrument became an end in itself.

Iran's story is further illuminating in its more recent events: a conservative "Guardian Council" headed by appointed clergy disqualified more than 2,000 of the reformist candidates for the national elections in February 2004. Many of those candidates were members of the clergy whose interpretations of their faith were very much at odds with those of the

Guardian Council. Even if the differences at some level were theological, obviously these differences were primarily manifestations of a political power struggle. Even if the differences reflected genuine debate about ideas, it is clear that Charles Krauthammer's point stands: religion can be interpreted in many different ways. Still, a critical question is how this debate will ultimately be settled: Will the resonance of ideas with the public be a factor in settling this debate? Or will the outcome be strictly a function of the relative political and institutional power of each group? Can the subjective interpretations of the powerful clergy subdue what are apparently differing societal interpretations of what is religious and what is ethical? This example highlights the need to discern the relationship between the religious and the ethical.

Faith versus Ethics

Two issues are central to the moral claims invoked in the name of religion, one pertaining to the internal perspective of the individual and the community of believers and the other to the external perspective of society at large. Is that which is religious also ethical? How does one differentiate the two? This has been the dilemma that has plagued many religious thinkers, but none gave answers as illuminating as those of the Danish philosopher Soren Kierkegaard in the latter stages of his writings. Here was a thinker who despised organized religion and struggled with the meaning and implications of his Christian faith. For much of his life, he believed that the ethical stage was the highest stage of being one can attain. Later, he came to the conclusion that there is another more profound stage, which he called *religious*. To understand the difference between the two, he tackled one of the Bible's most disturbing stories: God's instructing Abraham to sacrifice his beloved son. For Kierkegaard, this was an extraordinary choice between faith on the one hand and ethics on the other. That Abraham chose faith was for Kierkegaard the privileging of faith over ethics. That God ultimately reversed himself was the clear indication that God could never choose the unethical. For Kierkegaard, therefore, to be passionately faithful is to be passionately ethical.

This may be taken by some Christian believers to mean that their subjective faith, their interpretations of what God wills, determines what is ethical and gives them a moral high ground. But it is important to look carefully at the Kierkegaardian notion: while the subjective drive of an individual believer is strictly faith, the dilemma in the story arose in the first place because there was no doubt whatsoever, and by clearly external measures that are unrelated to the subjective faith, that sacrificing one's son was unethical. The happy ending of the story was happy only because of the knowledge that the external measures and the subjective drive ultimately coincided. There was no carrying out of the killing, only an expression of willingness. Had the killing taken place, an explanation of "higher ethics" would have been necessary to articulate the obvious gap emerging between religious behavior and common notions of ethical behavior. In this, there is a central lesson to be learned. Believers may have blind faith that their course is ethical, but the standard of the ethical must be constantly checked externally, for one may be having a delusion, not hearing the real voice of God.

That which is ethical should be recognizable by the external standards of society, not only by the subjective standards of the believer. For Kierkegaard, the difference between the purely ethical behavior and the religiously ethical behavior is the source of the internal drive: the natural passion of faith, on the one hand, and the habitual ethical behavior or that which is based on the fear of consequences, on the other hand. To be religious is to posit the self in terms that make ethical behavior a fulfillment of the self. The added value is internal, but the behavior is readily measurable by external ethical standards.

In his essay, Bryan Hehir emphasized the privileged position that Reinhold Niebuhr held in American foreign policy in the middle of the twentieth century. Although he had important theological influence within the community of believers, which enabled him to mobilize a great deal of support, his broader power in American society and politics was very much a function of his appeal to societal ethics beyond faith, in the process generating such support as existed among "Atheists for Niebuhr." This in turn re-enforced his theological power among the community of believers, for his standards of the ethical were external and internal.

Americans and others often make instinctive associations between the ethical and the religious. It is not surprising that our politicians often find it useful to be seen attending church or synagogue. The intuitive association may be that a religious person is more likely to be ethical than a non-religious person. In reality, the passionate faith a politician holds is an asset and a liability. If one does not agree with the behavior and policies of President George W. Bush but believes that this behavior is driven by deep religious faith, one is doubly troubled. If one's ethical standards match the behavior and standards of a Jimmy Carter, the knowledge that these decisions are principled and driven by deep faith makes them doubly attractive. Faith is often the source of the behavioral drive, but ethics is about the behavioral standards. Faith is appealing externally only when it is also seen as ethical from a societal point of view.

This brings me to my central point of agreement with Michael Walzer. In the end, the appeal to religious claims in our society cannot possibly determine what the moral course ought to be. Only broader societal ethical norms can be used as measures, even if, within any particular community of believers, the internal drive may be simply faith. But what constitutes the ethical?

What Is Ethical Foreign Policy?

The propositions advanced by Walzer about the obligations of governments in the conduct of their foreign policy sound eminently reasonable to me and, I am sure, to many others. The central question though is, who evaluates the extent to which one's actions conform to these propositions (or to any other set of propositions guiding ethical foreign policy)?

In the end, the primary criterion must be the degree of international consensus defined by several measures, especially with reference to international organizations, particularly the United Nations. This, to my mind, is the external test for the legitimacy of the internal drive: what we as a nation believe to be ethical and just, because of our own values or notions of interest, must always be checked against the assessment of the rest of the world.

Even in a world where international norms are less uniform and clear, and where power often trumps norms, ethical behavior cannot be defined solely according to the internal judgments of states. We may have faith that the internal ethical judgment of Americans, in the context of democratic decisionmaking, trumps the judgments of most other nations or existing international standards. But judgments that affect the interests of others, which allow no mechanisms of accountability involving those others, invite skepticism. In economic systems, we have little faith in the notion of a benign monopoly, just as we have little faith in the notion of a benign dictator in domestic systems. Monopolies and dictators may vary in their competence and individual standards; they are not all alike. But the problem remains: insensitivity, or even abuse, is unavoidable without external standards of accountability involving those parties affected by the actions of the powerful.

This is not to say that, as Krauthammer correctly points out, in international politics, the judgment of many actors, including international organizations could not be wrong sometimes, or that states that wield extraordinary power do not have the obligation to help define the ethical, to help shape international norms. But this relationship between an individual state's notion of ethics and an external world whose standards are in part a function of what the powerful actor will do requires conceptual separation.

As in domestic situations, an individual may have profound beliefs, religious or otherwise, that pit him against society's notions of the ethical. A conscientious objector, who believes that a war for which he is being drafted is unethical and may thus reject participation, will still be condemned by societal standards and punished. That he may accept his fate would be a reflection of his strong and impressive faith, but no one would allow such personal faith to define the ethical act for society. An individual can act as he may choose, but he is held accountable by the standards of the community. When an individual acts, his action affects not only himself but others in society, and thus he cannot be left without accountability for that action.

In considering the foreign policies of governments, the issue is not whether a state has the right, indeed as Walzer points out, an obligation, to serve the interests of its citizens above all else. Rather, the question is whether or not the state may disregard the interests of others who are significantly affected by its actions.

Powerful states have always understood that the existence of international institutions is better for them than their nonexistence. Most international institutions have been created not only for a common good but also especially for the interests of the powerful states. The norms of international institutions, including the United Nations, the International Monetary Fund, and regional organizations, disproportionately reflect the interests of their most powerful members. There is a difference between a state's using its power and influence to shape or change international institutions and norms and employing this power to completely disregard the very norms that it helped shape originally.

Sometimes moral ambivalence or indecision by international organizations and actors places a greater responsibility on the powerful states to "lead." But there is a difference in a powerful state's decision to take the lead and shoulder the burden on behalf of an issue on which there is support in principle, or mere indifference, and that state's taking the lead on behalf of an issue on which there is decided opposition. In confronting the Iraqi invasion of Kuwait in 1990, most states, including Japan and many European states, were initially reluctant to support a war to compel Iraqi withdrawal, although they believed that the occupation was illegal and should be reversed. The United States led, not by going against the strong opposition of others, but by using its power to persuade others to support the effort and pass appropriate UN resolutions. Certainly such "persuasion" sometimes entailed the employment of American resources, both incentives and threats, on a bilateral basis, to help build the coalition. And there was never a doubt about the justness of the cause according to accepted international norms. In fact the ultimate winning argument was normative: did smaller states want to accept the establishment of a post–cold war norm that legitimized the notion that a powerful state (Iraq) could at will invade a weak state (Kuwait)—and do so by defying the most powerful state of all?

A second example is the absence of intervention to stop genocide in Rwanda. The reluctance of the United Nations to intervene or at least to lead early and effectively is a matter that will continue to be debated. But one thing is clear: had the United States or another major power decided to lead and to carry the cost of intervention, most observers around the world would have applauded—even the ones who are almost always suspicious of American intentions. This would have been a war of choice, not necessity, but it would have been accepted by most countries as a moral choice.

A third example pertains to the U.S. intervention in Afghanistan to topple the Taliban regime and pursue al Qaeda. There were many around the world who doubted whether the United States produced enough evidence before the war linking al Qaeda with September 11, or whether America had given enough time to the Taliban to hand over al Qaeda leaders. But no one doubted America's right to respond forcefully to a horrific attack on its soil, and many states rallied behind the United States once the decision was made to wage war, and many previously unfriendly governments, such as those in Iran and Syria, cooperated in the critical arena of intelligence. Most people and states understand wars of necessity even if they do not like them. They have different views of what could justify wars of choice.

Contrary to conventional wisdom, the September 11 attacks and the early mobilization against al Qaeda brought America and much of the world together. It was the policy pursued after the collapse of the Taliban regime that began to drive a wedge between the United States and the rest of the world. The sense of empowerment that came out of the seemingly easy collapse of the Taliban inclined the Bush administration toward a more unilateral policy that many around the world found threatening to their vital interests.

These examples should be contrasted with the case of the Iraq war in 2003. By most measures, the effort was not accepted by international organizations or international public opinion. But the most troubling part was that many of those nations opposing American foreign policy were friends and allies who were not mere bystanders in another episode of discretion of a superpower (and history is full of those). Rather, the outcome of the war in Iraq was potentially more consequential to the most vital interests of states like Turkey, Iran, Jordan, Syria, Saudi Arabia, Israel, Kuwait, Arab states broadly, and the Europeans, than it was to the United States. To the extent that Saddam Hussein was seen to present an international threat, he was a greater threat to others than to the United States. What happens in Iraq in the post-Saddam era will affect the vital security interests of all its neighbors far more than it is likely to affect the security of the United States. The United States took upon itself the duty to define what is good for others, not only what is good for itself, or, in the view of many, America simply ignored the vital interests of others. Certainly, many Americans may have fully believed that they were performing an international good by removing the Saddam Hussein regime. But except in a self-righteous subjective way, it is hard to see how this action can be seen as ethical from an international perspective. External measures must always be the ultimate indicators of what is ethical.

Why an Ethical Foreign Policy?

For the individual, especially for a religious person, the drive to be ethical is part of the fulfillment of the self. The Kierkegaardian notions provide helpful clarifications. Recognizing that what drives ethical behavior is often mere habit or even fear of material consequences of unethical behavior, Kierkegaard believed that such motivation leads to disharmony within the self and ultimately to despair. Ethics must be sought as an end in itself, or better yet, as the consequence of a leap of religious faith, where the ethical becomes the natural behavior. I suspect that many religious and ethical individuals are driven by a sense of the ethical, not merely for its external consequences but for the personal comfort they attain when they look into the mirror every morning.

This internal drive can also motivate a community or a nation in its behavior toward other communities and nations. When one conceives of a nation as a unit existing among other nations, it is often true that the drive for ethical behavior originates in the fear that the internal values of a nation could otherwise suffer; citizens fear that unethical behavior abroad in part defines who they are at home, even in an international order whose standards are not uniform and are often difficult to discern. This is one source of the problem of the position advocated by Krauthammer that, because the international norms as he sees them are very far from the view articulated by Michael Walzer, policies that are unconstrained by such normative considerations are justified.

Yet, even aside from the disagreement about the role of norms in world politics, states often worry about the internal consequences of their external behavior. Take one of the powerful forces within Israel to end the occupation of the West Bank and Gaza: the fear that the unenviable role that young men and women play in controlling the lives of Palestinians has potentially devastating consequences for Israeli society itself. Similarly, many Palestinians worry that the horrific suicide bombing, even aside from its tragic consequences for Israelis, has a devastating effect on Palestinian society, especially in the glorification of death. In the United States, many voices that are heard objecting to the increasing discourse of confrontation between the United States and other nations, especially Muslim countries, worry that such discourse and policies may have a troubling effect at home on civil liberties. In raising support for military strategies abroad, there is always the fear that for many, especially the young, it is hard to separate the external from the internal norms. In the end one cannot fully defend one's values at home by subverting them abroad.

In short, the internal motivation of external ethical behavior is often a factor. But Krauthammer has a powerful point about how in a world where there is no central authority to enforce law and order, issues of national interest often supersede that which is deemed ethical by domestic standards. Moreover, material power, economic and military, remains a primary instrument of foreign policy in the relations among states. It is important to recognize the limits of this view, however, even before articulating its moral consequences. Ethical policy is consequential to notions of the national interest. A strong instrumental argument can be made on behalf of international ethical behavior.

There are serious consequences stemming from limitations on the unilateral deployment of power on behalf of a state's interests and values when that deployment is fully detached from the perceived interests and values of other states. Such limitations make it impossible to ignore the interests of others and still succeed. Because of the absence of clear international norms, the argument goes, the United States can act to advance its interests and values globally, since it is the most powerful state. America can thus advance such an important issue to it as democracy in Iraq, and ultimately the rest of the Middle East, by going to war to topple a dictatorship. Powerful as America is, it discovers that it still needs the help of others to accommodate U.S. forces, gain intelligence, and garner political support. The priority becomes winning the war, for losing it is not an option. Securing needed support becomes a higher priority than attaining democracy. If those who support America have to repress an angry public that is opposed to U.S. policies, the United States, even if it does so reluctantly, accepts that behavior, for, after all, vital interests always supersede other objectives in an anarchic world. After throwing out the dictatorship of Saddam Hussein, if America discovers that its presence is less accepted than expected, it still cannot afford to lose. The focus becomes defending U.S. troops and oil interests and preventing any outcome, even a democratic one, that may ultimately conflict with America's perceived vital interests. In the end, democracy is sacrificed even if it is the very value that America professed to advocate. And the United States becomes a weaker nation by virtue of losing more allies and spreading itself too thin. The ability to advance American values internationally is weakened. In the end, even the most powerful nation on earth is not powerful enough to always go it alone. The dilemma of power is that it is most useful when it is least used; the more one uses it, the less one has left to use, the weaker one's deterrence.

There are implicit international norms that significantly affect the utility of power. Our notions of vital interests and the notions of other states of their vital interests are affected by implicit international norms, such as the norm of sovereignty. These norms decidedly affect each nation's motivation in the pursuit of a particular policy and ultimately affect the utility of power. We take it for granted, for example, that our withdrawal from Somalia in the 1990s, after the tragic deaths of a small number of Americans, was a consequence of our public uproar. But what is implicit in this example is that our own public held notions of what is vitally important to America and the extent to which the loss of even one life could be weighed against the perceived interests. There can be little doubt that the United States had the capacity to stay and accommodate far greater losses as it did in places like Vietnam, but the question always pertains to the motivation of the American public weighed against the motivation of the Somalian adversaries for whom the outcome in Somalia was vital. In abstraction, it is reasonable to say that the United States is the most powerful nation on earth and thus has far greater opportunity than any other nation to achieve its objectives. In reality, norms of sovereignty define the degree of individual motivation, and the threshold of pain of each actor, in ways that significantly affect the effective exercise of power.

A more illuminating example comes from the Arab-Israeli arena. The contrast between Israel's experience in Lebanon on the one hand and its confrontations with Palestinians on the other may prove instructive.[2]

Israel withdrew from Lebanon in 1999 after years of occupation. Although the lesson learned by some in the region was that guerilla warfare works against Israel because of the perception that Israel was militarily defeated by the Lebanese Hezbollah group, the outcome was in large part a function of each party's motivation; each side's motivation was in turn a function of notions of the national interest that are informed by international norms. Militarily, Israel possessed overwhelming power compared with Hezbollah, the Lebanese state, and its domineering neighbor, Syria. Hezbollah forces numbered in the hundreds and had limited equipment. Israel not only had decisive military advantages but also inflicted considerably more pain on Hezbollah and on Lebanon (and sometimes on Syrian forces) than was inflicted on it. Because of Israeli actions, Lebanon suffered the creation of tens of thousands of refugees, hundreds of casualties, and the serious undermining of its economy through such methods as the destruction of power stations that paralyzed its capital, Beirut. In contrast, Israel's economy was minimally damaged by its presence in southern Lebanon, and the number of casualties it sustained was small by the measures of warfare (a few dozen a year). Israel could have afforded to continue its presence, and many within Israel's military establishment did not want to pull out of Lebanon without a peace agreement.

However, in the end, Israel did withdraw without such an agreement. Hezbollah members and others in the region interpreted this result as a military victory that could be replicated in the Palestinian areas. This conclusion was an erroneous and unfortunate interpretation. Israel's withdrawal and Hezbollah's success simply cannot be understood by the power equation alone or by the usual measures of winning or losing a war. At issue was each side's motivation. More important, the motivation was a function of two factors that are not directly related to power: the extent to which the conflict was seen by each side as vitally important to its existence and the extent to which the cause was perceived as legitimate in international eyes.

The fact that Israel occupied Lebanese lands and operated from them was seen by most Lebanese, including those who opposed Hezbollah, as a threat to their sovereignty that superseded any divisions among them. That there was no imminent threat to Israel's existence from Lebanon and that the Hezbollah guerillas largely focused their operations against Israeli troops on Lebanese soil raised questions in the minds of the Israeli public about the need to stay in Lebanon and about justifying even the smallest number of Israeli casualties. Had Hezbollah framed its objectives in terms of eradicating Israel rather than liberating Lebanon, and had it sent suicide bombers to kill Israeli civilians, Israel's motivation would have been significantly different. At a minimum, motivation affects each side's threshold of pain and will to exercise power. To achieve independence, Lebanon could endure immense pain; for no obvious vital interests, Israel could endure little. This issue of motivation is also affected by outside notions of the legitimacy of each side's cause: the sense that Lebanon's drive to seek independence was in harmony with the principles of sovereignty that most around the world accept generated more international sympathy for Lebanon than for Israel, which reinforced the determination of the Lebanese.

The Palestinian-Israeli confrontation in the West Bank and Gaza has been of a different nature. Here too Israel has had overwhelming military superiority. The Palestinians had even more motivation than the Lebanese because they had no state at all and were under occupation. Their threshold of pain has thus been very high because the issue is ultimately about existence. For Israel, three issues made the question of motivation significantly different than the situation in Lebanon: first, the proximity of the West Bank to the heart of Israel makes the outcome much more important. Second, a significant share of the Israeli population has always wanted to claim the West Bank as part of Israel. Third, the suicide bombings of civilians inside Israel have made the issue more vital because the threat is more immediate. As a consequence, even though the Palestinians have inflicted many more casualties on Israel than Hezbollah has, Israeli motivation has increased rather than diminished. Thus the balance of motivation on the Israeli-Palestinian front fuels the conflict even more intensely than the actual distribution of military power and reduces the chance that the conflict can be won through Palestinian attacks or through Israel's military superiority. Israel can inflict far more pain on the Palestinians than it suffers, but that is not the same as winning or achieving peace.

The obvious conclusion is that the success of a policy is not only, or even primarily in some cases, dependent on material power but also hinges on the strength of motivation for each side. Motivation is in turn very much affected by international notions of what is justifiable, especially by the norm of sovereignty. A policy that ignores such norms cannot ultimately succeed.

The success in confronting many of the threats to vital interest is highly dependent on the appeal to moral notions of what is internationally legitimate. Take the antiterrorism argument as an example.[3] Certainly, part of the war on terrorism is military confrontation with its organizers such as al Qaeda and its leaders, but that is not enough to win the battle. Terrorism is an instrument, not a movement, an immoral means employed by groups. Some of them have just causes, and some do not. To reduce its occurrence, terrorism must be internationally delegitimized and the conditions under which it thrives minimized. By definition, legitimacy and illegitimacy cannot be unilaterally decided. When the United States appears to go against the rest of the world, U.S. actions appear illegitimate.

The argument against terrorism is essentially moral: to dissuade others from using such tactics, one has to speak with moral authority. Those with legitimate causes who condone terrorism as a method to serve their ends see terrorism as a weapon of the weak and helpless who are facing a far stronger enemy. Around the world many people make the point that the definition of terrorism cannot be fully divorced from the degree to which the aim of the group is legitimate, and from the degree to which the power of the enemy it faces is overwhelmingly superior. Terrorism is seen as the weapon of the desperate and weak.

This notion should be challenged, as the United States has been trying to do: terrorist means must be rejected regardless of their aims. But any successful effort to reduce the appeal of terrorism must persuade people and groups not of the illegitimacy of the group's cause but of the illegitimacy of terrorist means. The argument is moral: the ends, no matter how worthy, cannot justify the means. The argument boils down to the notion that deliberate attack on civilian targets is unacceptable under any circumstances. But to persuade others of this worthy notion, those who make the argument must speak with moral authority. And for the argument to be more persuasive, others with moral authority must also use it. This tactic requires an appeal to societies and multilateral efforts to establish the notion of the illegitimacy of terrorist means.

Many of the most threatening actors in international relations today are nonstate actors, especially those that are transnational, particularly al Qaeda. Conventional military power works well to deter states, and America's military and economic might serves the United States well in deterring direct threat from any state or combination of states. But such power works less well in deterring dispersed nonstate actors. It is true that the clout the United States wields with states could be used to coerce others, or entice them, to help confront nonstate actors that are threatening to America. But there are considerable limits to what such a strategy can achieve. One needs a high degree of coordination in financial and intelligence arenas, which is much more difficult to manage strictly on a bilateral basis. And if the source of clout with the states is primarily coercive, it is much more difficult to get their wholehearted cooperation. Even their security services or financial institutions would provide only the absolute minimum they must, which often is not enough. Finally, in purely coercing other governments to help, the United States intensifies the gap between their positions and the position of their own populations, which in turn makes it harder for them to succeed in fighting nonstate actors. America's difficulties in Pakistan and Afghanistan today, despite the full and necessary cooperation of their governments, is a case in point.

The need for international norms and institutions has been understood to emanate from the selfish interests of powerful states. Even some of the most ardent realists have posed the argument about norms and institutions as long-term instruments in the service of interests that otherwise could not be easily managed. When the United States emerged as the most powerful nation after World War II, it understood that it could manage its interests in world affairs more easily and efficiently by constructing international institutions and norms, whose purpose would be to serve a common good but especially the good of the powerful states. Many realists viewed institutions such as the international monetary system, the United Nations, and the General Agreement on Tariffs and Trade as ultimately serving the interests of the United States while also benefiting others. Even if in any single episode in the short term, the United States was bound by norms and rules that restricted its behavior, the overall benefit of those norms and rules far outweighed their short-term costs. And when the overall cost rose, the United States and other powerful countries had the clout to modify these norms and rules within the existing institutions, not abandon them altogether.[4]

To summarize, arguments for an ethical foreign policy derive not only from the pursuit of ethics as an end in itself but also from its consequences for the interests that are said to drive behavior in the first place.

Is an Ethical Foreign Policy Possible?

The proposition advanced by Walzer that the invocation of the national interest in foreign policy is often a mere justification for a value-driven policy is not as provocative as it may seem at first. To begin with, the provocative side of the proposition is in part the juxtaposition of such a position with that of a supposed "realist" view. I think it is important to have clarity about what realists say, and more important, to differentiate realist views from the views of those that have come to be called "neoconservatives."

It is at once evident that there are significant differences between the two groups: whereas the neoconservatives universally supported the war with Iraq, most of the prominent realists in the American academy (Kenneth Waltz, Robert Jervis, John Mearsheimer, Stephen Walt, Thomas Schelling, Steven Van Evera, Robert Art, Richard Betts, and many others) opposed it. Neoconservatives are not realists.

Primarily, neoconservatives have one thing in common with most realists: the belief that material power remains the most important instrument of policy in the hands of states in a world with no central authority and that states remain the primary actors in international relations. The differences between them are more significant. Realists have always understood the limitations of power. They have generally believed that the aggressive deployment of power generates a balancing response from other states (thus the balance of power thesis). In contrast, neoconservatives adhere to the belief that the exercise of overwhelming power would generate a domino effect or a bandwagon effect of states that want to be on the side of the most powerful state. Whereas realists have been skeptical about the ability of powerful states to impose their values on other states, neoconservatives have long advocated the use of American power to spread American values abroad. Realists generally believe in the relative "rationality" of all states, in that they are first and foremost driven by the logic of survival and security. Neoconservatives, however, have questioned this realist assumption. Certainly, the most influential views in the Bush administration have been those of the neoconservatives, not the realists.

The views of realists are seen to be the most inconsistent with notions of ethical foreign policy. Yet realism is by no means a unified theory, and some of its most prominent adherents, such as Hans Morgenthau, conceived of moral dimensions of foreign policy even if they emphasized the primacy of material power in a world without central authority. Neorealists, led by Kenneth Waltz, conceived of their theories as providing descriptive, not prescriptive, propositions and differentiated between the aggregate relations among states, addressed by their theories, and the individual foreign policies of states. It is useful to articulate the implications of this view for the possibility of ethical international behavior and to assess its compatibility with Walzer's proposition that notions of interest sometimes provide mere justifications for "moral" behavior.

Even as descriptive propositions, realist views are prescriptively relevant: to say that states respond to threat by a tendency to seek a balancing response, not by falling like dominoes, is to reject the possibility that conquering Iraq will enable the United States to spread its influence and values simply by making an example of the Saddam Hussein regime. Realists predicted that the consequence of a unilateral war against Iraq would be the emergence of a coalition of states to prevent the possibility of more American unilateralism—not the sight of other states jumping on the American bandwagon. Thus, whatever one's goals in foreign policy are, the prescribed instruments cannot be derived without a sense of what is possible and what is likely.

Many realists, and certainly neorealists, believe that notions of *vital* interests, especially those pertaining to security, generally trump other values in the behavior of states. This is not to say that other societal values are not often important, but that the more in conflict these values are seen to be with vital interests, the more they are likely to lose. This view also has prescriptive implications: the optimism that America will make democracy a primary objective in its Iraq policy has already given way to realism. The American public is far more concerned today about potential losses in Iraq and the security of U.S. troops than it is about democracy in Iraq. Concern for the consequences of a democratic Iraq, ruled by Shiite clergy who may forge a close relationship with Iran and use Iraq's oil to project power, is a far greater concern in U.S. policymaking in post-Saddam Iraq than establishing democracy. These limitations, predicted by realist propositions, certainly affect the prescribed policies that are said to seek the spread of particular American values. The realist position here is derived not from a principled opposition to the spread of democracy but from an assessment of whether or not the prescribed policies are likely to achieve their intended consequences.

Neorealists have insisted that their theories pertain to trends in the relations among states over time, not to specific policies of individual states. Their theories address patterns of international relations but do not provide individual theories of foreign policy. Kenneth Waltz, whose name is often invoked with reference to realist rigidity on moral motivation of states, opposed the Vietnam war, the nuclear arms race, and even the 1991 war to liberate Kuwait because he did not believe that they served the national interest or were morally justifiable. The point is not the personal position of an important realist but the fact that many realists believed that much of American policy even during the cold war could not be explained by notions of the national interest and was motivated by ideology, domestic politics, or personal inclinations of American presidents.

At the heart of this realist view is a fundamental differentiation between the opportunities available to states, especially powerful states, on the one hand, and the motives of their behavior, on the other hand. Realism is much more a theory about international opportunities open to states than it is about the motives of states. The more powerful a state is, the more opportunity it has, the more likely it is that motives other than security are driving its foreign policy.[5]

Given the external opportunity, realism certainly does not preclude a role for internal motives, including moral ones. An example of a theory that envisions a domestic context allowing for such a role is Samuel Hunt-ington's notion of the American Creed and its impact on American for-eign policy.[6] One does not have to agree with Huntington's particular propositions about American foreign policy, but my point is that it is pos-sible to conceive of domestic circumstances providing a role for national or subnational values in foreign policy—given the international opportu-nity, which, for realism, is usually abundant for powerful states. Indeed, some of the main approaches to American politics envision a dominant role for interest groups that are often driven by group (though not always national) values, such as the Christian right, to name but one. Even eth-nic groups in America (Polish, Jewish, Cuban, Arab) are driven less by their own domestic political and economic interests and more by group values when they advocate particular foreign policies toward their ances-tral homelands. Nothing in realism precludes a theory, or an empirical finding, linking moral factors and the external behavior of states.

In the 2003 Iraq war, Walzer's view that the national interest is some-times invoked to justify policies that may be driven by "values" rings true. It also rings true for realists who opposed the war. The tragedy of Sep-tember 11 rallied the American public behind the president; it did not make the Iraq war necessary. The president had the opportunity to make any one of a number of cases: he could have just as easily asked the Amer-ican public to downgrade the Iraq issue in favor of building the most effective coalition against al Qaeda. It is unlikely that objective American interests, such as terrorist threats, or Middle Eastern oil, could have log-ically and automatically led to the conclusion that the Iraq war was nec-essary. There is evidence that the president and others around him sought to focus on Iraq even before September 11. His decision was the most critical: in times of severe crisis Americans rally behind the commander in chief.

Whether or not the president's decision was driven by his own sense of values, the politics of interest groups, or a true belief that the war was vital for America will have to await future investigation. But what should be readily clear is that the decision was contingent on the president's own belief. Even if this belief reflected personal values, it is highly likely that the National Security Council is now full of secret "findings" and "direc-tives" that explain the actions based on vital American interests, including oil, which will be ironically interpreted by future historians to mean that vital interests did indeed explain the Iraq war. Walzer has a strong point here, especially if by "values" driving the decisions he is not passing an ethical judgment about their content. Values can be misguided and self-defeating. Still, they often affect, maybe even determine, the foreign policies of powerful states facing fewer international restrictions. But such a notion of values should be differentiated from notions of international ethical behavior, which must always be evaluated externally.

Conclusion

An international system of state and nonstate actors without an effective central authority means that there are limits on states' ability to behave ethically. Despite that, nothing prevents the application of ethical standards in foreign policy—especially for powerful states—even as an end in itself. Moreover, there is much to suggest that the pursuit of primary interests cannot be optimally effective without ethical restrictions. Ethical standards must in the end be subject to measures beyond one's subjective interpretation of what is ethical.

In the American democracy, where passionate interest groups significantly affect policy, there is no reason why the moral issues of religious groups should not be driving forces in policy debates. Religious groups must be seen as legitimate interest groups in American politics, whose passionate commitment could ultimately affect the formation of domestic and foreign policy. But as in the case of other interest groups, which are always driven by their sense of what is important and good, the standards of societal and international ethics must be checked externally, for no group commands the moral high ground by virtue of its subjective beliefs.

Notes

1. See, for example, a survey by Associated Press conducted by IPSOS-Public Affairs, December 1–3, 2003, based on telephone interviews and a national adult sample of 1,001.

2. This example is taken from Shibley Telhami, *The Stakes: America in the Middle East* (Westview Press, 2004), pp. 171–74.

3. Ibid., chap. 1.

4. There is a prolific literature on "international regimes" that speaks directly to the utility of norms for powerful states from a realist perspective. See Stephen Krasner, ed., *International Regimes* (Cornell University Press, 1983).

5. For a full articulation of this view, see Shibley Telhami, "Kenneth Waltz, Neorealism, and Foreign Policy," *Security Studies*, vol. 11 (Spring 2002), pp. 158–70.

6. Samuel P. Huntington, "American Ideals versus American Institutions," *Political Science Quarterly*, vol. 97 (Spring 1982), pp. 1–38.

WHEN UNILATERALISM IS RIGHT AND JUST

CHARLES KRAUTHAMMER

THE EDITORS OF this volume asked: can religious convictions guide a moral foreign policy? Do they lead to fanaticism? I am not sure that question has any kind of answer. A Bible group I am in has just now reached II Kings. I can assure you that my first travel through Joshua was a revelation. For a book with a reputation of speaking to the deepest moral senses of humanity, Joshua is knee-deep in blood. I am sure one can find any message one seeks in the Bible, depending on where one looks.

An even more remarkable example, of course, is Isaiah 11:6: "The wolf shall dwell with the lamb, the leopard shall lie down with the kid, the calf and the young lion together; and a child shall lead them." What people do not know is that immediately before Isaiah speaks of the coming of the Messiah, "a rod out of the stem of Jesse," he speaks of one who "shall smite the earth with the rod of his mouth, and with the breath of his lips he shall slay the wicked." This is not all love thy neighbor.

Religion of course does not depend only on interpretations of scripture; traditions also count. But again, that does not answer the question of which way religion will incline someone on foreign affairs or any other issue. Which religious tradition and which strain are guiding adherents? Who speaks for Islam? Is it Osama bin Laden, or is it the kind of moderate universalism that we see in other parts of the world? Who speaks for Judaism? Is it the Meretz secularist party in Israel, or is it the Kach extremist party? So, I am not sure that the question of whether religious convictions guide a moral foreign policy is useful. Religion as an abstraction will not tell, inform, or guide anyone about how to act collectively or individually.

I was at a conference recently in which many people expressed apprehension and even offense at the president's invocation of religion in the 2003 State of the Union address in his discussion of Iraq and the coming war. One participant even spoke of "carrying the cross to Baghdad."

I think this apprehension is rather absurd. The American political tradition has long been suffused with a sense of providential history, from the least theistic of the founders, Thomas Jefferson, who four times invoked the deity in the Declaration of Independence, to, most famously and most beautifully, Abraham Lincoln, whose second inaugural was perhaps the most moving invocation of divine purpose in all American history.

The Bush invocation was very much in that tradition, and I think that the secular elites in America and the Europeans who are aghast at what they see as a God-driven cowboy have a total misunderstanding of the roots of that tradition.

The United States did not go to Afghanistan in order to Christianize. America went to civilize. And America's definitions of civilization are rather secular, deriving most directly from the Enlightenment, which itself was a reaction to religion. Now, some may have a spiritual impulse behind this civilizing mission, but that does not in any way make what the United States is doing a religious crusade.

I have some other thoughts about the editors' questions here, but I must say that I feel an obligation as the representative of a certain school of thinking to respond to three aspects of what Bryan Hehir and Michael Walzer have said.

The first is the critique of unilateralism and the notion, as I believe Hehir said, that multilateralism is the embodiment of a sort of a conservative tradition, which sees law-based multilateralism as the foundation of international order. The second point is the critique of preemption, and the third is what I see as a kind of utopianism in the presentations made.

I do not understand how in any way one can say that multilateralism in and of itself is morally superior to unilateralism. I do not see how numbers determine legitimacy. By that standard, Zionism is racism. An overwhelming majority of the United Nations said exactly that. I do not understand how we derive standards of legitimacy from multilateralism, or if one prefers, from the universalism in the United Nations.

Iraq was selected to chair the UN Disarmament Conference in May, and the chair after it will be Iran. For the UN Commission on Human Rights, the newly elected chair is Libya, a government that specializes in abduction, assassination, violent repression, and torture.

The United Nations, an Orwellian universe run by a majority, is the antithesis of international morality. To see the locus of international legitimacy in an institution as corrupt and disruptive as the United Nations is simply astonishing.

In fact, I disagree strongly with what Hehir said, that the foundation of order is multilateral action in international law. I think that is a fiction. It does not exist. The foundation of the current order in the world, the guarantor of the peace in just about every region, is power and, most specifically, American power. We live in a unique, unipolar international system. We have not seen this situation since the end of the Roman Empire, and I do not think we have adjusted our thinking to understand exactly what that means.

The peace in the Pacific Rim, the Persian Gulf, the Balkans, and in most of the regions in the world is a result, directly or indirectly, of American power or the threat of American power. And I think that in today's world, the fear and adjustment to that overwhelming power is the guarantor of security and peace. We saw that in Afghanistan. We are seeing it in the Persian Gulf. And we see it elsewhere in the world.

The idea that there is some multilateral structure, or some international law or agreement, keeping the peace is absurd. Do a thought experiment. Imagine the removal of the United States by some act of God from the world today and imagine how long international law and multilateralism would keep the peace in the Pacific, the Korean Peninsula, the Persian Gulf, the Balkans, or anywhere else in the world.

The idea of preemption is also critiqued in this volume. I suspect it is seen as an expression of the projection of American unilateralism but also as a doctrine. I think this opposition to a preemptive intervention is almost reflexive. The critique ignores the events of September 11, which I think should have illuminated how radically the world has changed—specifically that we now live in an age (perhaps we were living in it earlier, but we did not really acknowledge or understand it) of the distinct possibility of instant annihilation.

The knowledge of how weapons of mass destruction are produced has been democratized. And those weapons may spread into the hands of actors who are not deterrable and who are willing to die in the name of their cause. These actors are actively seeking and trying to acquire these weapons and will use them tomorrow if they acquire them today.

The world in which we could only be attacked by a foreign enemy mobilizing a land army whose progress would be slow and could be observed, and who could only attack very deliberately and obviously, no longer exists. It died on September 11, and if we do not understand that we live in a new world, we will suffer that instant annihilation, and then all of our debates about preemption will be rather beside the point.

Finally, I want to address Professor Walzer's ending remarks to the effect that the opponents of American unilateralism and opponents of the war in Iraq would be strengthened in their arguments if they would urge other actors in the world to bear the burdens in the advance of peace and security and humanitarianism.

I think he is right about that. But the fact that France and Russia are today acting out of a basic self-interest and that China has no interest whatsoever in the relief of the suffering of the people of Iraq tells us that to imagine that we are going to mobilize international world opinion in defense of the principles that we hold dear is a wan hope that will not be fulfilled. And if we await that kind of rescue from others, we will be waiting forever.

I do not understand in any way how we derive moral legitimacy for our actions, acting in the name of what we believe is right and humane and civilized, by getting the nod from the butchers of Tiananmen Square on the Security Council. I do not understand how the legitimacy of U.S. actions depends on the support and approval of Syria, which sits both on the Security Council and on the State Department's list of terrorist states.

There is a kind of absurdity in this reliance on others when we know how the others are acting. We know who they are, and we know that they are not guided in their actions in the world by anything remotely like the principles of morality and humanitarianism that are so important in guiding our own actions.

I would like to live in the world that Walzer has outlined. But that world does not exist. There is no prospect that it will exist in our lifetime. And in the face of the threat that we know exists, which we have seen on September 11, and which we know is threatening another September 11, we have no choice but to act unilaterally and by our own definitions of what is right and just.

"MORALITY IS REALLY HARD"

JAMES LINDSAY

B RYAN HEHIR MADE a point in chapter 1 worth stressing: religion is taking on increasing salience in world politics. If anything, Hehir underplayed how important this development is and how much it could complicate international relations in the future. Charles Krauthammer rightly pointed out that religious traditions are diverse. Different trends, strains, groups, and communities exist even within an individual religion. This diversity creates opportunities for division and conflict, especially in a globalizing world that is bringing people into closer contact.

The increased salience of religion is crucial because international disputes are hard enough to manage and resolve when they merely involve ordinary material issues. Another layer of complexity is added when those material issues take on a sacred cast. It becomes even more complicated to find ways to compromise and peacefully resolve conflicts.

Hehir was right to say we need to think a lot more about the impact of religion on world politics. This is going to be hard. We are not used to thinking about the topic. We do not have much practice handling religion, and the consequences of getting it wrong could be enormous. Moreover, it is crucial that we not make the mistake of thinking that religion's role in world affairs simply involves frictions between Christendom and Islam. A major flashpoint today and for the foreseeable future is Hinduism versus Islam in South Asia, which has rightly been described as one of the most dangerous places on the earth, if not the most. And as I've already mentioned, conflicts can arise within religions as well as between them. Just think of the tensions between Sunni and Shiia in Iraq.

Hehir also brought up the erosion of sovereignty. Under the Westphalian state system, states are sovereign within their borders. Other nations are supposed to respect those limits. In the past several decades, though, that norm has eroded. More support now exists for intervening in other countries to prevent ethnic cleansing, avert humanitarian disasters, and oust tyrants. But the international community has yet to agree on the rules of the road to govern such interventions. Complaints are made that some interventions are simply unjustified or are efforts by the powerful to impose their will on the weak, who can do nothing about it. At other times intervention is hailed as a great triumph of the evolution of the international system. So it is an issue that deserves more discussion.

The third point I want to respond to in Hehir's presentation is about the Bush administration's national security strategy. I doubt it is as transformative as he suggests. I also am not sure that the administration's emphasis on preemption, which Krauthammer discusses, rises to the level of a doctrine. It clearly is not as easy to do as is sometimes suggested.

One candidate for preemption would be North Korea. As Krauthammer has recognized and discussed at great length in his recent columns, preemptive military action against North Korea is very difficult to do. Even under the best conditions it could lead to the deaths of thousands of American soldiers, not to mention thousands of Koreans. This is not to argue against the notion of preemption; it is simply to point out that it cannot be the sole basis on which one builds a foreign policy.

Furthermore, no one in the American political arena seriously argues that the United States does not have a right to act preemptively against terrorists. The real issue has to do with a handful of rogue states. And as the North Korean case suggests, here there can be strong prudential reasons for deciding against preemption.

Now to address the editors' question about whether religion can guide foreign policy. People should keep in mind that most Americans, regardless of their faith or even whether they have a faith, tend to think of foreign policy in moral terms. It is also important to recognize that America's face to the world is represented not just by what the U.S. government does abroad but also what individual Americans do. In this respect, I mention the very long-standing missionary movement in the United States. One can go all the way back to 1806, to the haystack prayer meetings outside Williams College in Massachusetts, which led to large numbers of missionaries—mostly Protestant missionaries during the nineteenth century, subsequently supplemented by Catholic missionaries, Adventist missionaries, and missionaries from the Church of Latter Day Saints among others—going overseas and proselytizing. Depending on one's perspective, they performed many great deeds—one can point to the creation of Robert College in Turkey or the American University in Beirut—or they committed ignoble acts—one could think, for instance, of the role missionaries played in the American seizure of Hawaii.

My point is that nongovernmental actors, or transnational actors, as Hehir describes them, existed long before IBM and General Motors. They were exporting American values and ideas, and in the process they won friends and created enemies for the United States.

But back to the question of what the U.S. government does abroad. Part of the problem that plagues our dialogue about foreign policy is that we are trapped by our talk about liberals versus realists. Krauthammer, I believe, situates himself as a realist. In this formulation liberals are the ones who are interested in morality, and realists are assumed to have no interest in morals. After all, they are the ones presumed to be interested in raw, hard power. The truth, however, is something different. Most Americans, including many who would proudly call themselves realists, do take moral considerations into their calculations.

Americans are particularly uncomfortable with raw, pure realpolitik. Henry Kissinger's tenure as national security adviser and then secretary of state is a case in point. His approach to foreign policy generated many critics, but they came from the left and the right. Although they may have disagreed on the specifics of what Kissinger got wrong, they were united in one thing—that Kissinger's belief that statesmen should put moral consideration aside when making foreign policy was wrong. Critics on the left complained that Kissinger's policies helped to keep oppressive, authoritarian governments in power. Kissinger's critics on the right argued that his policy of détente failed to face up to the evil of the Soviet Union and communist regimes.

The tendency, then, of Americans to think in moral terms is not the province of one part of the foreign policy spectrum. Nor is it tied to any particular religious denomination, which leads me to Michael Walzer's comments about the morality of war in Iraq. They remind me of a conversation I had with a graduate student when I was teaching and using Walzer's *Just and Unjust Wars.*[1] The student came up after class and said, "You know what, Professor Lindsay? Morality is really hard." And I said, "Well, if it were easy, do you think Professor Walzer would have written such a long book?"

This point about complexity is often lost when we discuss the morality of foreign policy. There is a first-order problem here, namely, which actions are moral? What is our moral code? As Walzer discussed in his book, being a consequentialist or utilitarian means evaluating means in terms of the ends they achieve. But it is possible to choose instead to be an absolutist and believe that certain means can never be justified regardless of how good the end is. But the complexity of moral action goes beyond which moral code to choose. Moral calculations are inevitably tied to pragmatic calculations about the way the world works and what the consequences of actions will be. They are also tied into calculations about probability of events, as Walzer quite rightly pointed out.

Even individuals with coherent moral philosophies can on the same issue at different points in time come up with different answers. Walzer had a stimulating essay in the *New Republic* in September 2002 analyzing whether the Bush administration was justified in going to war in Iraq. His argument was essentially the one we are hearing now. But as he frankly acknowledged in the essay, he had a different view on it in the mid- to late 1990s, largely because in his judgment the circumstances at that time were materially different.[2] Others would, and have, disagreed.

At the same time, considerable uncertainty surrounds which policies would work and which would not. Take the argument for containment. Perhaps Saddam Hussein could be contained. But then again, perhaps not. Or containment might work for a while and then collapse over time. To be fair to President George W. Bush, the reason UN inspectors returned to Iraq is that he threatened to use force. Countries that had been sitting on the sideline or wanted the problem just to go away—and Krauthammer eloquently pointed out that many countries look to duck tough problems—suddenly got religion, so to speak, and decided that heightened containment was preferable to war. But if Bush had not put the threat of war on the table, containment would likely have continued to have deteriorated, an outcome that very few people, regardless of their moral persuasion, wanted.

The points about complexity and consequences also apply to Walzer's discussion of foreign aid. Walzer correctly notes the importance of broadening the circle of winners in the international society. It does not automatically follow, however, that the answer to third world poverty is a doubling of foreign aid or a mass transfer of resources. Economists and political scientists have pored over the data on foreign aid for years in an attempt to figure out whether aid promotes growth. Many studies suggest that on balance it is a wash or, if anything, that aid can inhibit economic growth.

My point is not to criticize foreign aid. My point, rather, is that we all have a tendency to simplify complex issues and look for simple solutions. In the particular case of broadening the circle of winners, we need a strategy far broader than one that says send money overseas. For starters, the developed world also needs to change its trade policies and to reduce agricultural subsidies. Developing countries also have many steps to take, including reducing corruption, establishing the rule of law, and empowering all their citizens.

In closing, I do appreciate the tendency of Americans to cast their policy preferences in moral terms. That tendency, however, can squelch debate. When people become certain of their moral rectitude, they can easily drift into sanctimony, so anybody who disagrees with them must by definition not be really interested in moral issues. That attitude tends to poison the debate rather than advance it.

The lesson here is that we all could benefit from a bit of humility and respect when it comes to debating the morality of foreign policy. Morality is a fuzzy compass for charting a wise course for the United States abroad. None of us has a monopoly on moral calculation. And the world we so wish to master has a habit of confounding even our most deeply held moral beliefs.

Notes

1. Michael Walzer, *Just and Unjust Wars: A Moral Argument with Historical Illustrations*, 3d ed. (New York: Basic Books, 2000).

2. Michael Walzer, "Inspectors Yes, War No. No Strikes," *New Republic*, September 2002, pp. 19–22.

CONTRIBUTORS

E. J. DIONNE JR. is a senior fellow in Governance Studies at the Brookings Institution and University Professor in the Foundations of Democracy and Culture at Georgetown University. He is a syndicated columnist with the *Washington Post* Writers Group and a co-chair, with Jean Bethke Elshtain, of the Pew Forum on Religion and Public Life. Dionne is the author of *Stand Up Fight Back: Republican Toughs, Democratic Wimps and the Politics of Revenge, Why Americans Hate Politics,* and *They Only Look Dead.* He is editor or coeditor of several Brookings books including *Community Works; What's God Got to Do with the American Experiment?; Bush v. Gore; Sacred Places, Civic Purposes;* and *United We Serve.*

KAYLA MELTZER DROGOSZ is a senior research analyst for the religion and civil society project at the Brookings Institution and visiting faculty fellow for the Center for Democracy and the Third Sector at Georgetown University. She received her degree from New College in Sarasota, Florida, continued her graduate studies in religion at Hebrew University, and received an MPA from the Maxwell School of Citizenship and Public Affairs at Syracuse University. She served previously with the policy offices of United Jewish Communities and in the political section of the U.S. Mission to the United Nations.

JEAN BETHKE ELSHTAIN is the Laura Spelman Rockefeller professor of social and political ethics at the University of Chicago. She is a member of the National Commission for Civic Renewal and currently serves as chair of both the Council on Families in America and the Council on Civil Society and as co-chair, with E. J. Dionne Jr., of the Pew Forum on Religion and Public Life. Elshtain is the author or coeditor of many books, including *Just War against Terror: The Burden of American Power in a Violent World, Jane Addams and the Dream of American Democracy, Who Are We? Critical Reflections and Hopeful Possibilities, Democracy on Trial,* and *Public Man, Private Woman.*

FATHER BRYAN HEHIR is the Parker Gilbert Montgomery Professor of the Practice of Religion and Public Life at Harvard's Kennedy School of Government. Before his tenure as president and CEO of Catholic Charities USA from 2001 through 2003, he served as dean of the Harvard Divinity School and at the U.S. Catholic Conference of Bishops. He was a member of the Vatican Delegation to the United Nations General Assembly and the U.N. Special Session on Disarmament and an adviser for U.S. Bishops at the Extraordinary Synod of Bishops in Rome. His publications address the ethics of strategy and politics, as well as the role of Catholic social thought.

CHARLES KRAUTHAMMER is an essayist and syndicated columnist. His *Washington Post* column appears in more than 130 newspapers worldwide. Krauthammer writes a monthly essay for *Time* magazine and contributes frequently to the *Weekly Standard,* the *New Republic,* the *National Interest,* and other journals. His columns have been awarded the Pulizer Prize for distinguished commentary; his essays, the National Magazine Award for essays and criticism. A graduate of Harvard Medical School, he is a recipient of the Bradley Prize and of the Irving Kristol Award of the American Enterprise Institute.

JAMES LINDSAY is vice president, director of studies, and Maurice R. Greenberg Chair at the Council on Foreign Relations. Previously, he was deputy director and a senior fellow in Foreign Policy Studies at the Brookings Institution, professor of political science at the University of Iowa, and director for Global Issues and Multilateral Affairs at the National Security Council. A consultant to the Hart-Rudmann Commission, Lindsay has authored or coauthored numerous books, including *America Unbound, Agenda for the Nation, Protecting the American Homeland, Defending America,* and *Congress and the Politics of U.S. Foreign Policy.*

LOUISE RICHARDSON is executive dean of the Radcliffe Institute for Advanced Study at Harvard University. She was an associate professor, as well as head tutor, of Harvard's Government Department. While at Harvard, she was awarded the Levenson Prize, given by the undergraduate student body to the best teachers at the university, and the Abramson Award, presented annually to a Harvard faculty member for excellence and sensitivity in teaching undergraduates. An expert in international terrorism, international relations theory, and British foreign policy, Richardson is the author of *When Allies Differ* and has contributed to several journals and books.

SHIBLEY TELHAMI is a nonresident senior fellow at the Brookings Institution and the Anwar Sadat Professor for Peace and Development at the University of Maryland, College Park. He is a member of the Council on Foreign Relations. He previously held positions at Columbia University, Cornell University, and Princeton University, among others. His publications include *The Stakes: America and the Middle East*, *Identity and Foreign Policy in the Middle East*, and *Power and Leadership in International Bargaining*. He has contributed to the *Washington Post*, *New York Times*, *Los Angeles Times*, *Baltimore Sun*, and *Foreign Affairs*, among other publications.

MICHAEL WALZER is a professor of social science at the Institute for Advanced Study in Princeton. He writes about political and moral philosophy and has played a part in the revival of a practical, issue-focused ethics, and in the development of a pluralist approach to political and moral life. His current project is a series, *The Jewish Political Tradition*, that has thus far produced two volumes: *Authority* and *Membership*. Walzer is coeditor of *Dissent* magazine and a contributing editor to *The New Republic*. Previously, he taught at Princeton and Harvard Universities. He has written many books, including *Arguing about War* and *Just and Unjust Wars*.

INDEX